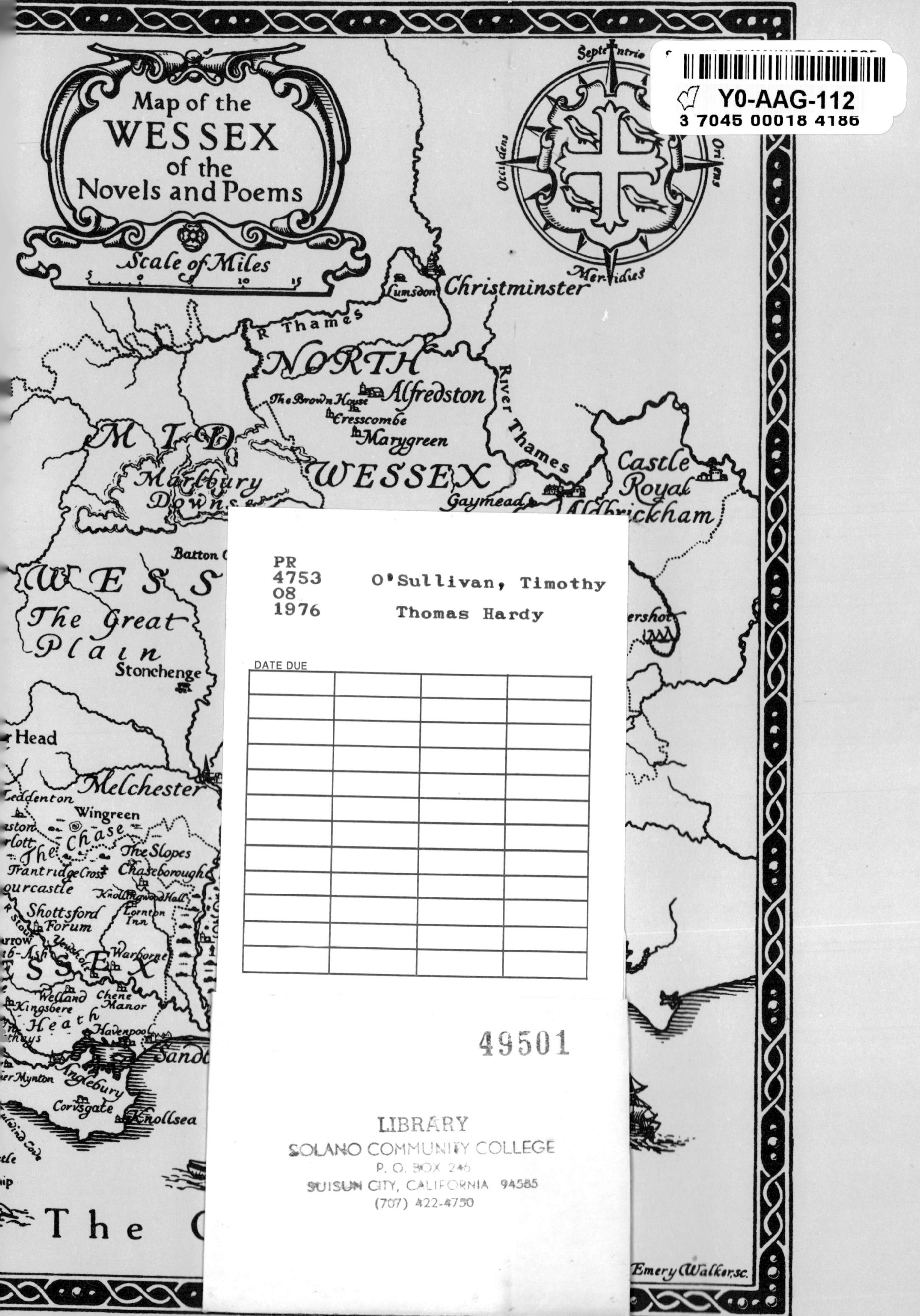
Map of the
WESSEX
of the
Novels and Poems
Scale of Miles
Christminster
Lumsdon
R Thames
NORTH
Alfredston
The Brown House
Cresscombe
Marygreen
River Thames
MID
WESSEX
Marlbury
Downs
Castle
Royal
Gaymead
Aldbrickham
Batton
The Great
Plain
Stonehenge
Melchester
Leddenton
Wingreen
The Chase
The Slopes
Chaseborough
Trantridge Cross
Knollingwood Hall
Shottsford
Forum
Lornton
Inn
Warborne
Welland
Chene
Manor
Kingsbere
Heath
Havenpool
Anglebury
Corvsgate
Knollsea
The
Emery Walker sc.

# THOMAS HARDY

# THOMAS HARDY
## An Illustrated Biography
Timothy O'Sullivan

St. Martin's Press
New York

*St. Martin's Press, Inc., 175 Fifth Ave., New York, N.Y. 10010*

*Printed in Great Britain*

*Library of Congress Catalog Card Number: 75-27159*

*First published in the United States of America in 1976*

# Contents

## Acknowledgements

ALL quotations, unless otherwise specified, are from F. E. Hardy's *The Life of Thomas Hardy, 1840-1928* (Macmillan, 1962). For permission to use other material by Hardy and his second wife Florence, I have to thank the Trustees of the Hardy Estate.

For help with the preparation of the book, including permission to use illustrations where they are attributed in the List of Illustrations on pages 186–7, I am indebted to: Her Majesty the Queen, Mr N. J. Atkins, Miss Francesca Barran of the National Trust, Mrs Enid Bown, Lord David Cecil, Mr Robert Cooke, M.P., Mr K. V. Cooper, Mr Nicholas Cooper of the National Monuments Record, Miss E. A. Evans of the National Portrait Gallery, Miss Anne-Marie Ehrlich, Mr James Gibson, Mr Richard Graves, Miss Evelyn Hardy, Miss Margaret Holmes and Mrs Janet Hudson of the Dorset County Record Office, Mr Michael Holroyd, Canon W. R. Houghton, Mrs Vera Jesty, Mr K. W. Lamb of the Birmingham Museum and Art Gallery, Mr Charles E. Lee, the Rt Hon. Harold Macmillan, Sir Robert Mackworth-Young, Professor J. C. Maxwell, Mr D. P. Mayne of the Imperial War Museum, Professor Michael Millgate, Mr E. J. Nevitt of the Royal Hospital, Chelsea, Mr Roger Peers and the staff of the Dorset County Museum, Mr D. Pepys-Whiteley, Mr F. B. Pinion, Mr Michael Pitt-Rivers, Miss Gillian Pitts-Tucker, Professor J. K. S. St Joseph, Mr and Mrs J. P. Skilling, Mr John Sparrow, Messrs James and Gregory Stevens-Cox, editors of the *Thomas Hardy Year Book*, and Mrs Anna Winchcombe.

Most of all, I should like to thank Miss Caroline Hobhouse of Macmillan London Ltd for her interest in the book.

TIMOTHY O'SULLIVAN

## Chronology

1840 Thomas Hardy born at Higher Bockhampton, near Dorchester. His father and grandfather were builders, also keen performers in the instrumental choir of the local parish church.

1848 Attended school established by his local patroness Julia Augusta Martin. About this time his mother gave him Dryden's *Virgil*, *Rasselas* and *Paul and Virginia*.

1849 Transferred to school in Dorchester. Played fiddle at local weddings and dances.

1856–61 Articled to Dorchester architect, John Hicks. Studied Latin and Greek in his spare time and began writing verse. Was introduced to modern thought by his friend Horace Moule, son of the Vicar of Fordington.

1862–7 In London, working for the architect Arthur Blomfield. Read widely; studied paintings in National Gallery; began to alter the basis of his inherited religious beliefs.

1867–70 Returned to Dorset for health reasons and was employed by Hicks, and his successor Crickmay, on church restoration.

1868 Completed draft of first novel, 'The Poor Man and the Lady' (later destroyed).

1870 Sent by Crickmay to St Juliot in Cornwall and met future wife, Emma Lavinia Gifford. Writing *Desperate Remedies*, his first published novel.

1873 Invited by Leslie Stephen to contribute serial (*Far from the Madding Crowd*) to *Cornhill*.

1874 Married and took rooms in Surbiton.

1876–8 Living at Sturminster Newton; writing *The Return of the Native*.

1878–81 Living in London. Was becoming well known in literary circles. Had a serious illness while writing *A Laodicean*.

1881 Took a house at Wimborne Minster.

1883 Went to live in Dorchester.

1885 Moved into the house, Max Gate, in Dorchester, which he had built for himself. He and his wife continued to make long annual visits to London.

1888–91 Writing many short stories. Publication of *Tess of the d'Urbervilles* in 1891 created furore.

1892 His father died.

1892–4 Worsening relations with his wife, the trouble being exacerbated by the writing of *Jude the Obscure*. In 1893 they visited Dublin and met Mrs Henniker, with whom he collaborated on a short story and perhaps fell in love.

1895–6 *Jude* published, causing scandal. He resolved to give up novel-writing.

1897–8 Writing and revising poems for his first collection, *Wessex Poems*.

1902 Began *The Dynasts*.

1904 His mother died.

1910 Received the Order of Merit.

1912 Making final revision of the Wessex novels. His wife died in November.

1913 In March made penitential pilgrimage to St Juliot and later to his wife's birthplace, Plymouth. Wrote flood of poems 'in expiation'.

1914 Married Florence Dugdale. At outbreak of war joined group of writers pledged to write for the Allied Cause.

1914–28 Wrote and revised the material for several more collections of verse.

1928 Died. His ashes were buried in Westminster Abbey and his heart in his first wife's grave in Stinsford churchyard.

WHEN Thomas Hardy was born there on 2 June 1840, the hamlet of Higher Bockhampton was a lonely spot at the edge of Puddletown Heath. To the south and west, woodland gave way to the Frome Valley around Lower Bockhampton and Stinsford, three miles downstream from Dorchester. All were wrapped in their own peculiar silences.

In 1840 the ways of the heath, the valley and the woodland were separate. Dorchester was the inward-looking centre of them and of innumerable similar settlements in south Dorset. Any wider unity rested on a common indifference to the world outside, superstition and the festive but serious observance of cults with roots less traceable than those of the Established Church. But it was an unsettling time: less than ten years before Hardy's birth, the trade union martyrs from the nearby village of Tolpuddle had dignified the notion of organisation among the peasantry; before he was eight the railway had rent the Frome Valley, overturning the customs and working conditions of centuries; and by the time he was a young man the comfortable beliefs of the literate were being shaken from the laboratory and the pulpit.

The Hardys' house at Higher Bockhampton, c. 1900. The surroundings had been gradually cultivated since Hardy's grandparents moved there in 1801. Hardy's earliest surviving poem, 'Domicilium' written when he was about eighteen, incorporates what his grandmother had told him about her first years there. It ends:

*'Our house stood quite alone, and those*
*tall firs*
*And beeches were not planted. Snakes*
*and efts*
*Swarmed in the summer days, and*
*nightly bats*
*Would fly about our bedrooms.*
*Heathcroppers*
*Lived on the hills, and were our only*
*friends;*
*So wild it was when first we settled here.'*

Hardy described his family as having all 'the characteristics of an old

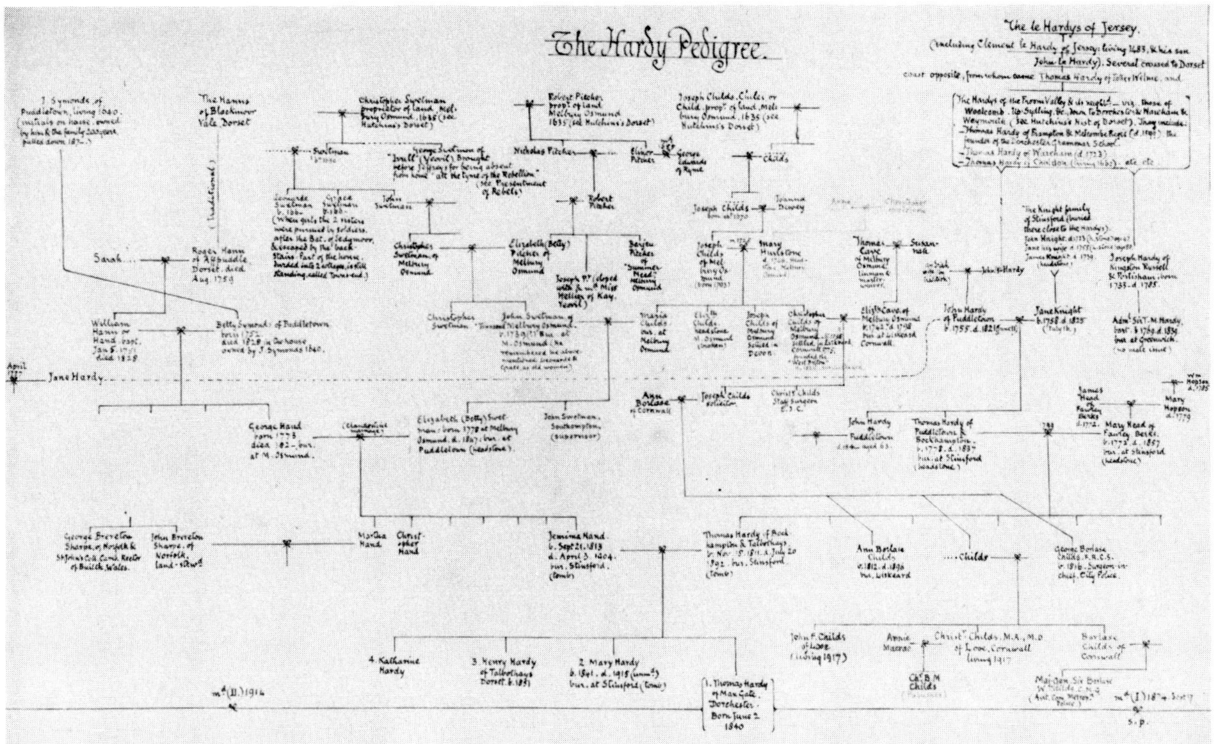


The Hardy pedigree in Thomas Hardy's handwriting

## The Pedigree

I

*I bent in the deep of night*
*Over a pedigree the chronicler gave*
*As mine; and as I bent there,*
*half-unrobed,*
*The uncurtained panes of my window-*
*square let in the watery light*
*Of the moon in its old age:*
*And green-rheumed clouds were hurrying*
*past where mute and cold it globed*
*Like a drifting dolphin's eye seen*
*through a lapping wave.*

II

*So, scanning my sire-sown*
*tree,*
*And the hieroglyphs of this spouse*
*tied to that,*
*With offspring mapped below in*
*lineage,*
*Till the tangles troubled me,*
*The branches seemed to twist into a*
*seared and cynic face*
*Which winked and tokened towards*
*the window like a Mage*
*Enchanting me to gaze again*
*thereat.*

III

*It was a mirror now,*
*And in it a long perspective I*
*could trace*
*Of my begetters, dwindling backward*
*each past each*
*All with the kindred look,*
*Whose names had since been inked*
*down in their place*
*On the recorder's book*
*Generation and generation of my mien,*
*and build, and brow.*

IV

*And then did I divine*
*That every heave and coil and*
*move I made*
*Within my brain, and in my*
*mood and speech,*
*Was in the glass portrayed*
*As long forestalled by their so*
*making it;*
*The first of them, the primest*
*fuglemen of my line,*
*Being fogged in far antiqueness past*
*surmise and reason's reach.*

V

*Said I then, sunk in tone,*
*'I am merest mimicker and*
*counterfeit! –*
*Though thinking,* I am I,
And what I do I do myself
alone.'
*– The cynic twist of the page*
*thereat unknit*
*Back to its normal figure, having*
*wrought its purport wry,*
*The Mage's mirror left the*
*window-square,*
*And the stained moon and drift*
*retook their places there.*

family of spent social energies', and its history was the basis of his lifelong interest in genealogy. It seems to have given him sentimental satisfaction. Rather, as he followed the developing science of genetics, some recurrent feature of his ancestry – what is called in the poem 'Family Portraits' 'My blood's tendance' – troubled him, and different aspects of heredity play a part in much of his most sombre work. Incest, an inevitable consequence of sexual mishaps over several generations in a small community, or persistent incompatibility in marriage, or mere illegitimacy may have been the problems. If Hardy knew of instances among his immediate forebears, he chose not to show them in the various pedigrees he drew up. These are simplified, claiming descent from the le Hardys of Jersey and, among the mainland branch, kinship with Thomas Hardy of Melcombe Regis, who had endowed Dorchester Grammar School in the sixteenth century, and Sir Thomas Masterman Hardy, Nelson's captain of *Victory* at Trafalgar.

When or why Hardy's own branch of the family declined, or whether they lived continuously in Dorset at all, is not known. By the end of the eighteenth century his great-grandfather John was a builder in Puddletown, prosperous enough to establish his son in the same trade and build the house at Bockhampton for him and his daughter-in-law, Mary Head of Great Fawley in Berkshire. They moved in in 1801. The son, who was the first of three generations of Thomases, prospered in his building work, which included the bridge at Lower Bockhampton, trained as a volunteer to face the invasion by Napoleon expected in 1803-5 and continued a family tradition by leading the Stinsford church choir. Of their three sons, Hardy's father, Thomas II, was born in 1811.

Hardy's maternal grandmother Elizabeth Swetman came from a family of middling yeomen, settled since the seventeenth century at Melbury Osmund in north-west Dorset. Although she lived nearby in Puddletown and did not die until he was seven, Hardy had no personal memory of her. In her youth she had been a handsome woman of much promise, well dressed, highly literate and famous locally for her medical knowledge, which she used to improve traditional remedies. But she married, against her father's unrelenting wishes, George Hand, who held an uncertain position in life between shepherd and general labourer, and when he died his widow and children became a Poor Law family. Hardy's mother Jemima, born in 1813, made the most of it by reading every book she could lay hands on, but her early years cast a permanent shadow over her life and she grew up determined that no child of her own should ever feel its chill.

Jemima spent much of her childhood in Puddletown. Later she worked for the Earl of Ilchester at Melbury House and in London but was back in Dorset when she first set eyes on Thomas II

(*above*) Thomas Hardy I's account for building the O'Brien vault in Stinsford church.
Lady Susan O'Brien, a daughter of the first Earl of Ilchester, disgraced herself by marrying the Irish comedian William O'Brien, a protégé of Garrick. 'Even a footman were preferable,' noted Horace Walpole. Nevertheless, they lived a devoted married life for years at Stinsford House, next to the church. When O'Brien died, Lady Susan asked Hardy's grandfather to build the vault 'just large enough for our two selves only'.
Although she died in 1827, Lady Susan's memory was still warm in Hardy's childhood. 'She kept a splendid house', one of her old workmen told him, ' – a cellarful of home-brewed strong beer that would almost knock you down; everybody drank as much as he liked. The head gardener was drunk every morning before breakfast. There are no such houses now!'

(*below*) Townsend, the Swetmans' house at Melbury Osmund, from a sketch by Emma Hardy, 1887. Hardy's story 'The Duke's Reappearance' was based on a family tradition that the Swetmans harboured the Duke of Monmouth there after the battle of Sedgemoor in 1685.

From the Day-book for 1815 of T. Hardy, builder. Bockhampton, born 1778 died 1837.

Mr. O'Brien's Vault ※

To 1 Day making Morter

Septr. To 3 Days taking up the pavement in the Chancel

& examining the ground & cleaning Pavement — 8 — 0

To 5 Days digging the Vault & wheeling out the earth — 0

To 8 Days walling & paving the Vault & making benches & whitewashing &c. & filling in the Earth behind the walls & walling under the foundation of the Chancel — 1 — 1 — 4

To 4 Days covering the Vault & paving the chancell & cleaning the Church — 7 — 0

To 8 Days Labourer — 11 — 0

To 5 Sacks Lime

N.B. 1 Sack of Lime not Used — 3

16 To 1 Day making good the paving in Chancel

1 Day [illegible]

10 Quart of Beer [illegible]

[illegible] — 4 — 10 — 0

※ This was Wm. O'Brien actor & dramatist, whose elopement with Lady Susan Strangways in 1764 was famous. The vault (in which she was also afterwards interred) is under the chancel of Stinsford Church. (See Walpole's Letters & Dic. Nat. Biog.)

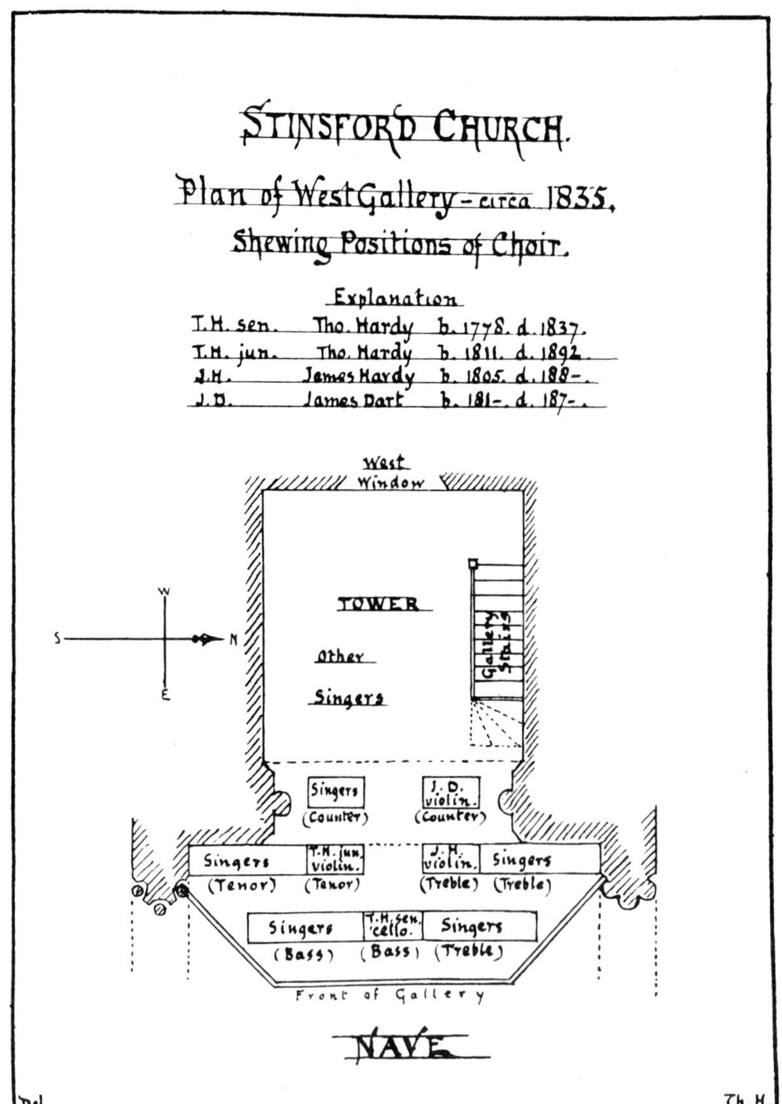


A Church Romance
*(Mellstock: circa 1835)*

*She turned in the high pew, until her sight*
*Swept the west gallery, and caught its row*
*Of music-men with viol, book, and bow*
*Against the sinking sad tower-window light.*

*She turned again; and in her pride's despite*
*One strenuous viol's inspirer seemed to throw*
*A message from his string to her below,*
*Which said: 'I claim thee as my own forthright.'*

*Thus their hearts' bond began, in due time signed.*
*And long years thence, when Age had scared Romance,*
*At some old attitude of his or glance*
*That gallery-scene would break upon her mind,*
*With him as minstrel, ardent, young, and trim,*
*Bowing 'New Sabbath' or 'Mount Ephraim'.*

playing the violin in the gallery of Stinsford church. More than three years passed before their marriage in December 1839, which was evidently precipitated by the conception of Thomas III, born five months after the wedding. They had three other children: Mary, born in 1841, Henry in 1851 and Katharine in 1856. None of them married, and as both Hardy's own marriages were childless his branch of the family became extinct on Katharine's death in 1940. By reason of their nearness in age, but also because of her very solemn temperament, Hardy was closest to his elder sister. For many years Mary was headmistress of Dorchester Girls' National School, where Katharine also taught. As the portraits of her parents in the Dorset County Museum show, she was a more than competent painter and was also the most gifted musically of the four, serving as organist in several parishes throughout her active life.

At birth, Hardy was thrown aside as dead by the doctor but rescued by the nurse. He remained fragile, and until he was five or six his parents doubted whether he would survive childhood. Unlike his friend Edmund Gosse, whose entry into the world was equally perilous, Hardy never expressed any gratitude for this deliverance. One of the earliest experiences which he chose to remember was an occasion, recalled in 'Childhood among the Ferns' and a scene in *Jude the Obscure*, when he lay in the sun reflecting on the life he had known and deciding that he did not want to grow up. But he was not a morbid or unhappy child. He was of an 'ecstatic temperament', intensely perceptive of his surroundings, enthralled by the music of language and, according to 'The Self-Unseeing', literally entranced by the rural ditties and dances which, before he was very old, he had learned to accompany on his violin.

The standing of his family at Bockhampton was secure and comfortably above most of their indigenous neighbours. 'Veterans' Valley', as the lane in which they lived was known locally, housed two retired army officers and others of a semi-genteel origin on whom the Hardys did not jar. The Dorset dialect, used for dealing with the workmen and people who knew no other tongue, was not spoken at home. The subtleties of the family's position had been accentuated by Thomas I's leadership of the Stinsford church choir. His fellow musicians were poor and thirsty men, and in the course of their activities much drink was consumed at the Hardys' expense. The seven-roomed house and one and a half acres of land were only lifehold, but the Hardys owned property elsewhere which, at the death of Thomas II in 1892, included a farm at Talbothays, brick-kiln, yard and a dozen or so cottages. Much of the building work was provided by the estate of Francis Martin of Kingston Maurward House; but when, owing to an imagined slight, this was placed in

Mary Hardy, aged about fifteen. The poem 'Conjecture' suggests that Hardy's favourite sister meant as much to him in some respects as either of his wives. Yet she was a painfully self-effacing character. Hardy wrote on the day of her funeral in November 1915: 'As Mr Cowley [the rector of Stinsford] read the words of the psalm "Dixi, Custodiam" [XXXIX] they reminded me strongly of her nature, particularly when she was young: "I held my tongue, and spake nothing: I kept silence, yea, even from good words." That was my poor Mary exactly.'

other hands, Thomas II readily found comparable work farther afield. The question of moving to larger and more convenient premises in Dorchester where the business, which already sometimes employed as many as fifteen men, might have developed was often discussed in Hardy's childhood, but Thomas II 'had not the tradesman's soul' and nothing was done.

Although Thomas II was assiduous enough at his trade to be carried along by the building boom of the fifties and sixties he cannot, in his wife's view, have been a provident influence over their children. Both the Hardys and the Hands were large families and few of their members enjoyed or aspired to the vestiges of gentility of the Bockhampton household. Jemima's brothers at Puddletown in particular had none of their sister's squeamishness about the simpler pleasures of life, and while her two younger children kept her much at home until she was in her middle forties, Thomas II fitted comfortably into their society of an evening. When he was still very young Hardy sometimes went with him to play the violin. Evenings which, like the Saturday night outing of the Trantridge workers to Chaseborough described in *Tess of the d'Urbervilles,* began as convivial would become drunken and thereafter sometimes orgiastic. Hardy never said what he must have seen as he stood aside, stone sober, waiting to steer his father home across the heath to be greeted by some stern words of reprobation from Jemima.

Thomas III was thus brought up in circumstances which made him strongly aware of social differences. He soon learned more on his own account: initiating the Stinsford children in the wonders of salvation at the Sunday school; acting as amanuensis to their elder sisters pursuing their sweethearts in the army; and, as the early favourite of Francis Martin's childless wife Julia Augusta, absorbing something of a fairer world.

Throughout his life, every feature of Hardy's surroundings spoke to him, In his seventies he told Clive Holland that 'ideas frequently presented themselves to his mind in the first instance more as mental pictures than as subjects for writing down'. In visual terms the surroundings in which he grew up could hardly have been richer or more varied. Downland, forest, meadowland and heath ornamented by earthworks marking the slow progress of man against nature, and churches and manor-houses built in some of the finest English stones were all almost within view of Bockhampton. Hardy believed in the oneness in essence of nature and man. One of his most serene, if bizarre, poems 'Voices from Things Growing in a Churchyard' describes the characters of the dead living again in

(*above*) The living-room in the Hardy's house, where Thomas listened to his grandmother's memories of Great Fawley and of Dorset under the threat of invasion by Napoleon, and first heard the Stinsford church-choir's secular repertoire.

The Self-Unseeing

*Here is the ancient floor,*
*Footworn and hollowed and thin,*
*Here was the former door*
*Where the dead feet walked in.*

*She sat here in her chair,*
*Smiling into the fire;*
*He who played stood there,*
*Bowing it higher and higher.*

*Childlike, I danced in a dream;*
*Blessings emblazoned that day;*
*Everything glowed with a gleam;*
*Yet we were looking away!*

(*below*) Hardy with his mother, 1841

plants fed by their decomposing bodies. But in life men too often defiled and frustrated the work of nature.

Although his own home circumstances were closer to those of *Under the Greenwood Tree* than of *Tess of the d'Urbervilles,* Hardy was fully aware of the hopelessness and brutality of the lives of many of the peasantry around him. When he was accused of darkening the country scene in his novels, he replied that if he had told the whole

(*above*) Hardy's father at the age of sixty-six

(*right*) Kingston Maurward House built, in brick, by Thomas Archer for George Pitt, 1717–20. Morton Pitt ruined himself facing it in Portland stone to impress George III in 1794. It was the home of Francis and Julia Augusta Martin, 1845–55, and the model for 'Knapwater House' in *Desperate Remedies*.

truth no one would have stood it, and in view of the outcry against both *Tess* and *Jude the Obscure* he was no doubt right. Scenes like Jude Fawley's introduction to Arabella by way of a slap from a pig's pizzle, or Robert Creedle's dismissal of the slug in Grace Melbury's cabbage – 'He was well boiled' – cannot have been entirely artistic in origin. But in his essay 'The Dorsetshire Labourer' Hardy was careful to point out the difference between such a lack of fastidiousness and true squalor, and to emphasise the advantages – stability, intimacy and working conditions which, however cruel, were purer than those in the factories – of rural life. That was in his youth. By the time the essay was written in 1883 there was far more misery on the land, brought about by changes ruthlessly enforced from outside and the end of lifeholds – tenures granted for three lives – established during the eighteenth-century enclosures. Labourers had less security of tenure, and as a result they let their cottages and gardens decay around them; the morality of migrant workers polluted questionable but secure conventions, and the rootless usages of their speech destroyed dialects.

With migrant workers came other developments subversive of traditional life. When, around 1850, a horse-drill was wheeled into the corn-market at Dorchester, the labourers whose forebears had scattered the seed by hand for a thousand years stood bemused, wondering who could have thought of bringing such a thing among them. Later innovations, such as the steam threshing-machine described in chapter 47 of *Tess,* entered the countryside like creatures from Hell, tyrannising the lives of people accustomed to serve 'vegetable, weather, frost, and sun'.

These elements were themselves hard enough masters. Hardy's evocation of Talbothays dairy in *Tess* may suggest an idyll, but he was there describing the gentlest type of agricultural work in ideal

Discouragement

*To see the Mother, naturing Nature, stand*
*All racked and wrung by her unfaithful lord,*
*Her hopes dismayed by his defiling hand,*
*Her passioned plans for bloom and beauty marred.*

*Where she would mint a perfect mould, an ill;*
*Where she would don divinest hues, a stain,*
*Over her purposed genial hour a chill,*
*Upon her charm of flawless flesh a blain:*

*Her loves dependent on a feature's trim,*
*A whole life's circumstance on hap of birth,*
*A soul's direction on a body's whim,*
*Eternal Heaven upon a day of Earth,*
*Is frost to flower of heroism and worth,*
*And fosterer of visions ghast and grim.*

(opposite) Inside a Dorset Cottage towards the end of the nineteenth century.

Dorset farm workers
*'. . . it is among such communities as these that happiness will find her last refuge on earth, since it is among them that a perfect insight into the conditions of existence will be longest postponed.'*
(From Hardy's essay 'The Dorsetshire Labourer', written in 1883.)

conditions. Those who, like Tess and the other Talbothays dairy-maids, drifted down to field labour could be condemned to the bitter drudgery of reed-drawing or swede-grubbing in an open field where the 'rain had no occasion to fall, but raced along horizontally upon the yelling wind, sticking into them like glass splinters till they were wet through'.

Life, however beastly, was pathetically fragile. Hardy never forgot the feel of the weightless body of a starved fieldfare frozen to death on a winter's day nor ceased to revile what he described to Sir George Douglas as the 'contingencies of a world in which animals are in the best of cases pitiable in their limitations'. He once wrote a poem following the strangulation of a cat in a rabbit wire, 'The Death of Regret', so powerful that it was changed to apply to a person. He saw two hangings in Dorchester, but because men had a little more control over their fate than animals the casual extinction of the victims' lives touched him comparatively little. Seventy years after the execution of Martha Brown, witnessed from a place immediately below the scaffold, all he could remember was 'what a fine figure she showed against the sky as she hung in the misty rain, and how the tight black silk gown set off her shape as she wheeled half-round and back'. On his own unanswerable terms, he took the notion of the oneness of nature beyond the limit. In the course of a correspondence arising from his opposition to blood sports, he once suggested that 'there would appear to be no reason why the smaller children, say, of overcrowded families, should not be used for sporting purposes. Darwin has revealed that there would be no difference in principle; moreover, these children would often escape lives intrinsically less happy than those of wild birds and other animals.'

We Field-women

*How it rained*
*When we worked at Flintcomb-Ash,*
*And could not stand upon the hill*
*Trimming swedes for the slicing-mill.*
*The wet washed through us – plash, plash, plash:*
*How it rained!*

*How it snowed*
*When we crossed from Flintcomb-Ash*
*To the Great Barn for drawing reed,*
*Since we could nowise chop a swede –*
*Flakes in each doorway and casement-sash:*
*How it snowed! . . .*

'Flintcomb-Ash', where Tess Durbeyfield worked as a field-woman

(*above*) Stinsford church which remained dear to him long after his disenchantment with Christianity. In 1924 he wrote to the rector from Max Gate, in a neighbouring parish: 'Yes: regard me as a parishioner certainly. I hope to be still more one when I am in a supine position some day.'

Afternoon Service at Mellstock
*(Circa 1850)*

*On afternoons of drowsy calm*
*We stood in the panelled pew,*
*Singing one-voiced a Tate-and-Brady psalm*
*To the tune of 'Cambridge New'.*

*We watched the elms, we watched the rooks,*
*The clouds upon the breeze,*
*Between the whiles of glancing at our books,*
*And swaying like the trees.*

*So mindless were those outpourings! –*
*Though I am not aware*
*That I have gained by subtle thought on things*
*Since we stood psalming there.*

(*below*) Popular vilification of Napoleon included this 'corpse head', published in 1815

Hardy learned to read almost before he could walk. He became bookish to such a degree that everybody said he would have to be a parson. The possibility of ordination was not finally abandoned until he was twenty-five, and he never lost an affection for some of the simple certainties of his churchy childhood. His formal education was little more than basic, but both before and after he left school he pursued further knowledge by himself obsessively. If this background led to a certain parrotry of allusions and references in his work, it also helped to develop an exceptional memory which was useful to him as a novelist and vital as a poet. Not only events but the nuances of emotions would remain clear in his mind for fifty or more years, ready to be recalled for a poem.

For the first seventeen years of his life, until her death at the age of eighty-five, Hardy's paternal grandmother Mary lived in the minute room next to the one used by Hardy and his brother Henry. She would have been in her seventies before he was much aware of her and by then, according to 'One We Knew', lived in the past, dwelling on her childhood as an orphan at Fawley and the early years of her marriage with Thomas I. A lot of what she told him, including some personal detail, eventually went into *Jude the Obscure*. The heroine of 'The Alarm' was based on her: she had been about to give birth to her son John when Thomas I and the volunteers were mobilised to meet Napoleon in 1803 and no doubt trembled more than most, if she believed the rumour that the invader daily ate the flesh of a new-born child for breakfast. The invasion, of course, never came, but Mary Hardy had kept some of the lurid propagandist literature of the time, as well as her memories, and between them they started her grandson on a lifetime's study of the epoch which led, by way of *The Trumpet-Major*, to *The Dynasts*.

In the next generation Jemima Hardy, although reticent about her ghastly childhood, 'was a woman with an extraordinary store of local memories, reaching back to the days when the ancient ballads were everywhere heard at country feasts, in weaving shops, and at spinning-wheels', and Hardy learned them in their last hour, as they withered in the chilly wind of popular national culture blowing from London. She encouraged her son's reading and bought him books like Johnson's *Rasselas* and Dryden's *Virgil* with an eye to the future. She imbued him too with some of her fatalism. Hardy's notion of the blind, unfeeling and unthinking force which governs existence, the Immanent Will, can be traced to the simple beliefs of one brought up to feel the unchallengeable power of nature. 'Mother's notion (and also mine)', he noted in 1870, when he was fresh from reading Darwin, Spencer and Huxley, ' – that a figure stands in our van with arm uplifted, to knock us back from any pleasant prospect we indulge in as probable.'

Hardy became the precocious favourite among the village children

(*left*) Jemima Hardy, aged sixty

(*below*) The School built by Julia Augusta Martin at Lower Bockhampton, which Hardy attended in 1848–9

of Julia Augusta Martin, and perhaps with him in mind she built and endowed a school at Lower Bockhampton. He was its first pupil, arriving on the first day even before the teachers; but by 1849, when he had outgrown his earlier delicacy, Hardy was thought fit enough to go to the British School in Dorchester. So, for the next five years or so, he walked the three miles into Dorchester and back every day, passing the squalid purlieu of Fordington, which harboured the *demi-monde* of the pompous county-town, along with paupers, criminals and disease, which included a bad outbreak of cholera in 1854. Mrs Martin was very displeased by the removal of her prize pupil, not least because the Dorchester school was nonconformist, but the reputation of its master Isaac Glandfield Last transcended sectarian prejudice and attracted many pupils from the surrounding area and later from farther afield, when a second school was opened for boarders. Last seems to have been a bit of a tyrant, but Hardy flourished under him, learning Latin (an extra) and becoming seriously enough interested in Classics generally to teach himself Greek after he left. His fellow pupils found him a bit stuck-up, but Hardy was generally – to him even oppressively – popular; and as his character and intellect developed he began to find their comparatively simple company tedious.

If Hardy had stayed at school longer, he might have gone straight into the Church, but in 1856 he caught the eye of the Dorchester architect John Hicks, who offered to take him as a pupil. Thomas II, who knew Hicks and respected his profession, thought the opportunity of establishing his son in it too good to be missed. So for the next few years Hardy continued to walk daily into Dorchester, usually with three or four hours' reading behind him in the early morning, up High East Street and turning left opposite St Peter's Church into South Street, where Hicks had an office at number 39. Hicks was a sympathetic employer, who shared Hardy's Classical interests and more than tolerated them as a distraction from work. He was a specialist in Gothic architecture, with a good provincial reputation as a church restorer; and, although Hardy later worked for some very famous architects in London, he thought a lot of his obscure teacher and dedicated 'The Abbey Mason', a whimsical account of the origin of the Perpendicular style, to him.

The other pupils in the office were more mature than Hardy, who, in his own words, was 'a child until he was sixteen', and better educated but willing to argue with him. When the clamour of a debate on some literary or religious point grew loud enough for Mrs Hicks to send down from her drawing-room to plead for peace and quiet, Hardy would slip next door, where William Barnes kept a school.

(*above*) Mill Street, Fordington. Hardy described it in *The Mayor of Casterbridge*:
*It was the hiding-place of those who were in distress, and in debt, and trouble of every kind. Farm-labourers and other peasants, who combined a little poaching with their farming, and a little brawling and bibbing with their poaching, found themselves sooner or later in Mixen Lane. Rural mechanics too idle to mechanize, rural servants too rebellious to serve, drifted or were forced into Mixen Lane.*

(*below right*) Hardy at about the time he went to work for Hicks

(*right*) High East Street, Dorchester

(*above left*) Isaac Glandfield Last's school in Greyhound Yard, Dorchester, where Hardy was a pupil from 1849. He probably left at the age of fourteen.

TEMPERANCE
HOTEL

(*opposite*) The screen between the south aisle and transept of Gloucester Cathedral, the oldest surviving example of Perpendicular architecture.
Hardy wrote 'The Abbey Mason' after a visit to Gloucester in 1911. The following year he told Sir Sydney Cockerell: 'what has struck me so often in relation to medieval art is the anonymity of its creators. They seem in those days to have had no personal ambition'.

Hardy and his sister Mary had loved the dialect poetry of Barnes from childhood, and his eccentric, patriarchal figure must have been familiar to them. Once Hardy got to know him, the friendship became as close as is possible between men separated in age by a generation and a half. Barnes had been born in very humble circumstances in the Blackmore Vale, and began to learn what eventually became an extraordinary number of languages and dialects while a clerk in a solicitor's office and to work slowly towards ordination, which he achieved at the age of forty-seven. 'A more notable instance of self-help', wrote Hardy, 'has seldom been recorded.' Not long after he got to know him, Barnes retired from his school to become Rector of Winterborne Came where, when Hardy moved into Max Gate, they were near neighbours. Hardy used to take visitors across the fields to hear Barnes preach long, unprepared sermons aimed exclusively at his small rustic flock, although by the time he died in 1886 he had an international reputation as a philologist. Barnes established the identity of the Dorset dialect among linguists and, by showing its very considerable charms in his lyric poetry, among a much wider audience. His achievement gave Hardy the confidence to articulate his own affection for the dialect in the mouths of some of his characters. It was Barnes, too, who resurrected the name of the Saxon kingdom of Wessex, which Hardy borrowed for the theatre of his novels.

Another more intimate but less equable friendship which developed while Hardy was at Hicks's was with Horace Moule, one of the eight sons of the Vicar of Fordington. Of Horace's brothers, Henry, the eldest, became Curator of the Dorset County Museum and a keen painter of the topography of Hardy's novels in watercolour; one became Bishop of Durham; another head of a Cambridge college; and the rest mainly lesser luminaries of the church and mission field. Like the Clares in *Tess of the d'Urbervilles*, the Moules were vigorously Evangelical and Horace, like Angel Clare, the nearest thing to a black sheep that such a family could ever produce. When Hardy got to know him well, he had survived an erratic career at both Oxford and Cambridge and was establishing himself as an essayist and critic. In Dorset, and to a lesser extent in London, they sought one another's company. Moule lent Hardy books and guided his precocious but untrained mind through the labyrinths of current religious and scientific thinking, in which Hardy originally responded more warmly to Newman than to Darwin.

(*below*) William Barnes

While acting as his mentor, Moule in no way encouraged Hardy to deviate from architecture. Indeed, in answer to a specific question about his future, he advised him to give less time to reading Greek and more to completing his pupillage in order to make a living from his profession as soon as possible. By this time Hardy

(*left*) Horace Moule

had written a few poems, of which only 'Domicilium' survives, but would have been powerless to make anything of himself as a writer. Throughout his life he was crippled by shyness: it made him almost incapable of initiating social contact or often of showing common civility, and probably accounts for some of his later reputation for snobbery and rudeness. But he was always more ambitious than he would admit. As soon as Hardy was enough of a celebrity to be lionised by fashionable society, its invitations were seldom refused, and as soon as he could afford it he regularly 'did' the London Season in order to make the most of them. So now, in 1862, when he knew enough about architecture to offer his services in a drawing-office more imposing than Hicks's, he went to London with an introduction to Benjamin Ferrey, a pupil of Pugin.

Hardy had been to London at least twice before – once with his mother on their way to visit an aunt in Hertfordshire, when they had stopped overnight at the hotel in Clerkenwell used by Shelley and Mary Godwin before their marriage, and once with his father on a day trip – but he knew very little of the city or its life. Many years later, in an address to the Society of Dorset Men in London – like most of Hardy's speeches, not actually delivered in person – he described a young man newly arrived from the country, seeing signs of his home county in the capital. As Hardy crossed Waterloo Bridge from the Dorset train in April 1862, he saw a townscape paved in Purbeck stone and dominated by Portland monoliths, from Somerset House ahead to St Paul's away on the right, and still very little of the iron and stock brick laid upon it during

(*below*) Hardy shortly before he left Dorchester to work in London

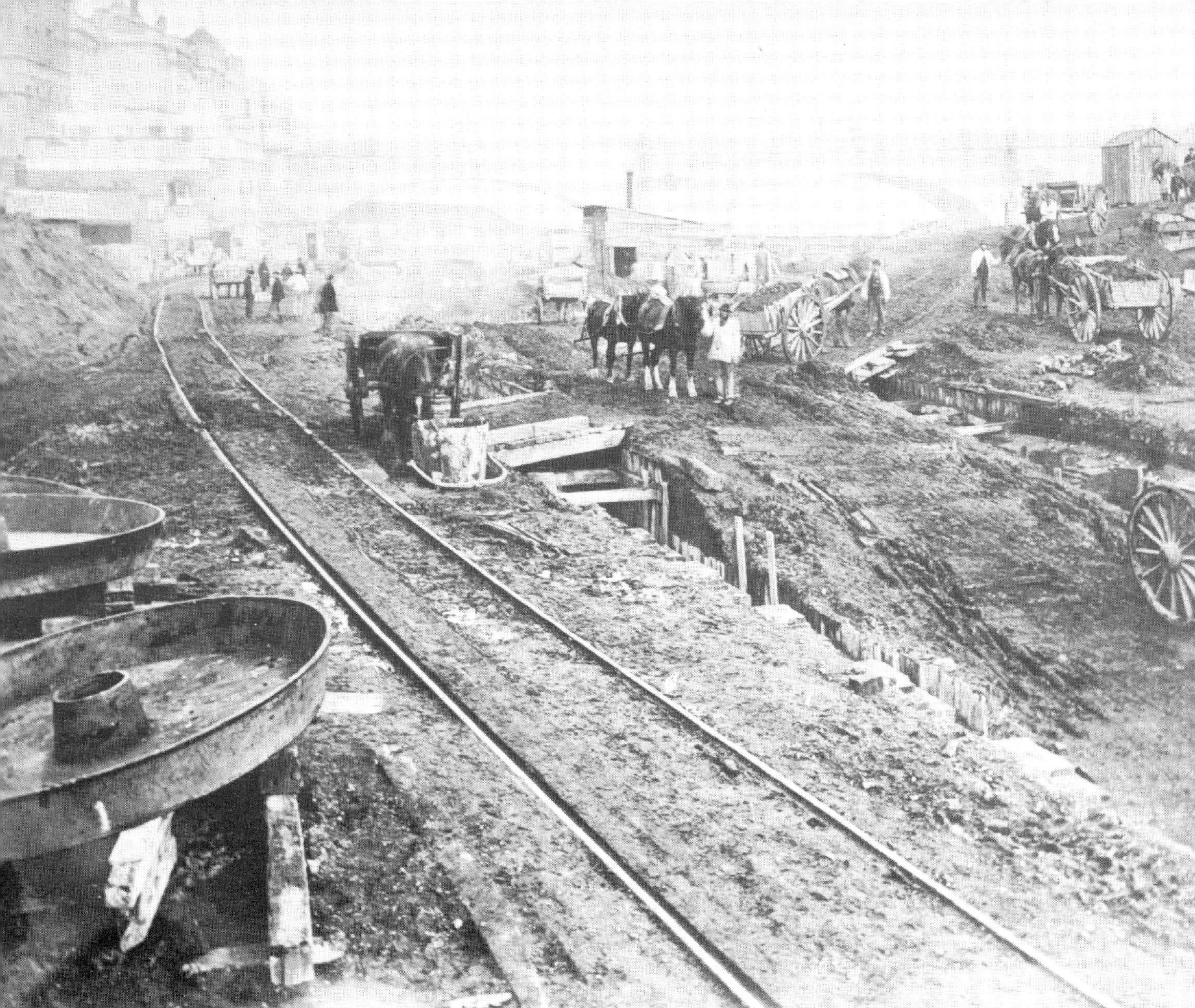

(*above*) The scene beneath the windows of Blomfield's office in Adelphi Terrace during Hardy's last few months there, when the District Railway was under construction

the next fifty years.

The introduction to Ferrey did not lead beyond an exchange of pleasantries, but another connection got Hardy a place in the office of Arthur Blomfield, where he worked for the next five years. The atmosphere there was as informal as it had been at Hicks's, although the pace of work required by Blomfield's large and fashionable practice was brisker. The office, in Adelphi Terrace, overlooked the Thames, which stank in summer, and towards the end of Hardy's time there conditions were made worse by the building of the District Railway and Victoria Embankment beneath the windows.

During his fifteen or so years in the profession, Hardy worked in London for Raphael Brandon and T. Roger Smith as well as Blomfield; and all three, although they have not worn well in taste by comparison with some of their contemporaries, were leaders of it in their time. Hardy himself was given a prize by the Royal Institute of British Architects for an essay 'On the Application of Coloured Bricks and Terra Cotta to Modern Architecture' and another by the Architectural Association, so he was evidently thought promising, but there is little work by which to judge his abilities. Two of the buildings on which he helped Blomfield – All Saints' Church, Windsor, and the chapel of the Radcliffe Infirmary, Oxford – do not belong to the class which would attract much of a clamour if it were now proposed to demolish them, but these, of course, were his employer's designs, not Hardy's. Both the buildings which he designed later – Max Gate for himself and Talbothays Lodge for his brother and sisters – are typical of many Victorian houses in being large without any feeling of spaciousness. Of the one and a half unexecuted church-designs that have been attributed to him, the incomplete one is remarkably like Blomfield's St Barnabas, Oxford, and the other similar externally to G. E. Street's church at Great Fawley. Hardy had sketched the old church at Fawley in 1864 and would have seen plans for the new one in Raphael Brandon's office, after Brandon had succeeded Street as architect to the diocese of Oxford.

One job, not of a strictly architectural nature, particularly interested Hardy. The Midland Railway was being extended into London to its new terminus at St Pancras. The route required a cutting through Old St Pancras churchyard and the removal of hundreds of coffins. Blomfield, the son of a bishop of London, was

The Levelled Churchyard

*'O Passenger, pray list and catch*
*Our sighs and piteous groans,*
*Half stifled in this jumbled patch*
*Of wrenched memorial stones!*

*'We late-lamented, resting here,*
*Are mixed to human jam,*
*And each to each exclaims in fear,*
*"I know not which I am!"*

*'The wicked people have annexed*
*The verses on the good;*
*A roaring drunkard sports the text*
*Teetotal Tommy should!*

*'Where we are huddled none can trace,*
*And if our names remain*
*They pave some path or porch or place*
*Where we have never lain!*

*'Here's not a modest maiden elf*
*But dreads the final Trumpet,*
*Lest half of her should rise herself,*
*And half some sturdy strumpet!*

*'From restorations of Thy fane,*
*From smoothings of Thy sward,*
*From zealous Churchmen's pick and plane*
*Deliver us O Lord! Amen!'*

Old St Pancras Churchyard

One of Hardy's two unexecuted church-designs. There is a similarity to G. E. Street's church in Great Fawley, Berkshire

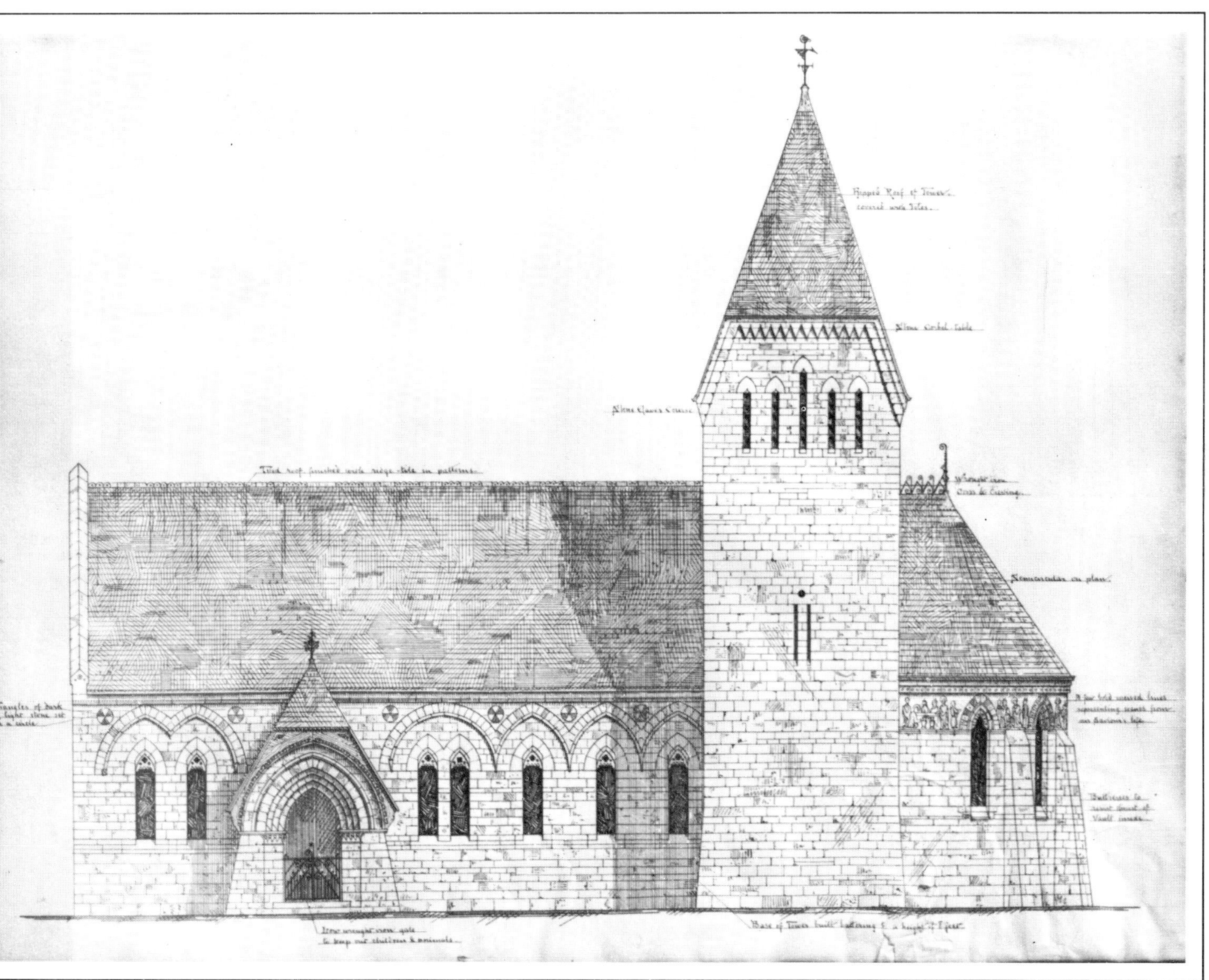

16, Westbourne Park Villas, Bayswater. Hardy lived there in 1863–7

considered a suitable man to ensure that the exhumation and re-interment were decorously performed and he chose Hardy to assist. The navvies, although fortified with liquor by the contractor, were nauseated by the stench and replaced by ripened gravediggers. Throughout the murky evenings of 1866, Hardy indulged a strong taste for anything to do with death in a veritable feast and gathered much graphic material for poems such as 'In the Cemetery' and 'The Levelled Churchyard'.

In London, Hardy lived first in the then leafy suburb of Kilburn and later at 16, Westbourne Park Villas in Bayswater. While maintaining a formidable reading programme, which for two years excluded all but poetry, in which he had decided was 'concentrated the essence of all imaginative and emotional literature', he made what he could of the frenzy of metropolitan life: music at Covent Garden; dancing at the Argyle and the Cremorne; and painting at the National Gallery, where he studied the work of one artist at a time, not allowing his eyes to stray on to neighbouring pictures. But he remained very solitary. Apart from Blomfield himself, he made no permanent friends in the office and few acquaintances outside it.

He wrote as well as read poetry. Many poems were sent to publishers, none accepted and some not even returned to him. In a letter to Swinburne in 1897, Hardy referred to these years as 'the buoyant time', but there is nothing light about the poems he wrote in his lonely lodgings. 'The Temporary the All', which he chose to open his first book of collected poems in 1898, set the tone of much of his poetic output, in speaking of the invariable denial of the promise of the future when the future becomes present. More specifically, in the circumstances of 1865, the poem refers to ambition blindly frustrated:

> Mistress, friend, place, aims to be bettered straightway,
> Bettered not has Fate or my hand's achievement;

'Hap', written the following year, asks why:

> ... How arrives it joy lies slain,
> And why unblooms the best hope ever sown?

While Hardy was not happy with his life as an architect and disappointed by the failure of his poetry, there were at least two more powerful sources of desolation: one was a loss of faith and the other was women.

Henry Robert Bastow, the pupil in Hicks's office who started Hardy thinking seriously about religion

By 1866 Hardy was as well prepared as most would-be ordinands to start training for the Church. Through the Moules he had made inquiries about going to Cambridge and also about entering Salisbury Theological College, but before anything could come of them his conscience had closed for ever the prospect of ordination and of the 'visioned hermitage' longed for in 'The Temporary the All'. The cheerless but stable rural fatalism on which he had been brought up did not withstand the ferment of the time or satisfy Hardy's desire for a pure conscience within it.

Henry Bastow, one of the pupils in Hicks's office, was a Baptist. During Hardy's time there he had announced his intention of being baptised and urged Hardy to do the same. Other temperaments, or even Hardy's own in a different age, might have regarded the advice as a piece of sectarian cheek, but in the wake of the Gorham controversy on the nature of baptismal regeneration he laboured over the question, reading all the polemical literature he could find and exercising the local clergy as they had never been exercised before. He was 'appalled at the feebleness of the arguments for infant christening' but 'incontinently determined to "stick to his own side", as he considered the Church to be, at some cost of conscience'.

Hardy's drawing for 'The Impercipient' in the first edition of *Wessex Poems* (1898) showing, from a distance, a congregation in the nave of Salisbury Cathedral, which as a building he admired more than any other

One doubt led to another, and the rootless thinking of the post-Tractarian Church left plenty of room for them. He followed Moule in examining the available apostasies, from Rome to atheism. He read Newman, 'because Moule likes him so much', and found the style of the *Apologia* 'charming, and his logic really human... Only – and here comes the fatal catastrophe – there is no first link to his excellent chain of reasoning, and down you come headlong.' Beyond theology, Hardy read and admired new and subversive books like *Essays and Reviews*, by some highminded and fastidious clergymen who were condemned and dubbed the 'Seven against Christ', and Darwin's *Origin of Species*, which undermined, partly by implication and partly by intent, every aspect of the Christian tradition, leaving Hardy largely shorn of his inherited beliefs. He remained churchy, 'not in any intellectual sense but in so far as instincts and emotions ruled and saying, in poems like 'The Impercipient':

> Why thus my soul should be consigned
>     To infelicity,
> Why always I must feel as blind
>     To sights my brethren see,
> Why joys they've found I cannot find,
>     Abides a mystery.

Under the stress of this crisis, the humid weather of the summer of 1867, hard work at Blomfield's and up to six hours' reading every day in his lodgings, Hardy's health began to fail. Blomfield told him to go to the country for a few weeks. He went home, leaving most of his books and other possessions at Westbourne Park Villas with a view to returning in October. In Dorset he soon recovered and resumed work for Hicks, but neither for the last nor the first time became innocently besotted with a woman.

Hardy was always vulnerable to beautiful women, Although his taste developed from village maidens to vicereines, he never forgot any of them and was fond of writing poems, like 'The Chosen', in which they are set as stars, splendid or blighted, in the firmament of his emotions. Some of the attachments were formed at an improbably early age. Elizabeth B——, for example, who was some years older, caught his eye around the age of twelve and remained a strong enough memory to be the subject of an affectionate poem, 'To Lizbie Browne', written at least thirty-five years later. Similarly Louisa Harding, the daughter of a rich Stinsford farmer, whom Hardy pursued in adolescence in the unchanging fashion of feckless

Louisa Harding. Hardy became infatuated with her when he was about fifteen. 'To Louisa in the Lane' was written when he was eighty-seven and she, who never married, had been dead and buried in Stinsford churchyard for twenty years.

*Meet me again as at that time*
*In the hollow of the lane;*
*I will not pass as in my prime*
*I passed at each day's wane.*
*– Ah, I remember!*
*To do it you will have to see*
*Anew this sorry scene wherein you have ceased to be!*

*But I will welcome your aspen form*
*As you gaze wondering round*
*And say with spectral frail alarm,*
*'Why am I still here found?*
*– Ah, I remember!*
*It is through him with blitheful brow*
*Who did not love me then, but loves and draws me now!'*

*And I shall answer: 'Sweet of eyes,*
*Carry me with you, Dear,*
*To where you donned this spirit-guise;*
*It's better there than here!'*
*– Till I remember*
*Such is a deed you cannot do:*
*Wait must I, till with flung-off flesh I follow you.*

infatuees, never to be rewarded with much beyond a shy smile then or thereafter, was longed for as a companion in the grave in a poem written during the last months of his life. Another, one Rachel – 'vain, frail, rich in colour and clever at artificial dimple-making' – was no subject for poetry; some of her characteristics were given to Arabella in *Jude the Obscure*. But Hardy never looked back on some of the more realistic passions of his twenties with the same composure. By that age, sex had become a menace to the tenacious respectability of Jemima Hardy's household. While his sisters scarcely left home except for the prison-house of a teachers' training college and Henry not at all, Thomas lived away alone and, armed with more desire than potency, was easily smitten.

(*above*) Henry Hardy, aged thirty
The younger Hardy children, Henry and Katharine, were simpler and more extrovert characters than Thomas and Mary. Henry, who followed his father into the building trade, retained a broad Dorset accent and habits to match, always preferring to tell the time by the sun rather than a watch.

The poems Hardy wrote in London are an anonymous but nevertheless vivid account of what happened. The first heresy on the road from pure emotion, untouched by experience, was a realisation of the evanescence of female beauty. Soon after he arrived in London in 1862, Hardy called on Mrs Martin and was aghast at what he found. The goddess whom he had worshipped at Kingston Maurward had degenerated into a commonplace middle-aged woman. 'Amabel' asked whether the love of his vision, a vision which he had carried in his mind for seven years, could inhabit this husk. The answer was no. At this stage in his thinking Hardy still had the consolation that the immortal soul at least was not a slave to time, but the soul soon proved equally inconstant.

A large number of the poems of these years, such as 'At a Bridal', 'Her Dilemma' and the 'She, to Him' sonnets, are either written from the purblind posture of an unrequited lover or are attempts to unravel the feelings of a woman racked by an emotional dilemma. His misery had no specific cause apart from contact with too many utterly inaccessible women. Some of Blomfield's more noticeable clients, or the not entirely innocent glitter of some of the ladies of the Cremorne, recognised thirty years later in 'Reminiscences of a Dancing Man', or actresses, who touched Hardy at his most vulnerable by idealising the idealised on the stage, tormented his imagination as he sat doodling in his lodgings, wondering 'what woman, if any, I should be thinking about in five years' time'. By 1866 he had had enough:

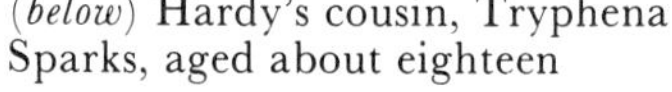

(*below*) Hardy's cousin, Tryphena Sparks, aged about eighteen

> Let me then never feel the fateful thrilling
> That devastates the love-worn wooer's frame,
> The hot ado of fevered hopes, the chilling
> That agonizes disappointed aim!
> So may I live no junctive law fulfilling,
> And my heart's table bear no woman's name.

It did not last long. When Hardy left Dorset in 1862, his cousin

In Vision I Roamed
To —

*In vision I roamed the flashing Firmament,*
*So fierce in blazon that the Night waxed wan,*
*As though with awe at orbs of such ostént;*
*And as I thought my spirit ranged on and on*

*In footless traverse through ghast heights of sky,*
*To the last chambers of the monstrous Dome,*
*Where stars the brightest here are lost to the eye;*
*Then, any spot on our own Earth seemed Home!*

*And the sick grief that you were far away*
*Grew pleasant thankfulness that you were near,*
*Who might have been, set on some foreign Sphere,*
*Less than a Want to me, as day by day*
*I lived unware, uncaring all that lay*
*Locked in that universe taciturn and dear.*

Tryphena Sparks was a child. When he returned in the summer of 1867, she had become a pleasant girl of sixteen who, unlike her sister Martha whom Hardy also liked, was serious enough to share some of his interests and young enough to be impressed by his comparative sophistication. Although Hardy expunged all but one explicit reference to Tryphena in his writing, her position as a pupil-teacher at the time he knew her best suggests that she was a mine for at least one of his characters.

For at least two years he saw her often, meeting in and around Bockhampton and Tryphena's home in Puddletown, and possibly later in Weymouth. From the autumn of 1869, however, Tryphena was firmly out of sight in Stockwell Training College, in south London, and a few months later was eclipsed in Hardy's mind by a quite different woman. If the poem 'At Rushy-Pond' refers to the end of the affair, it was evidently painful; but if Hardy jilted her he seems to have thought very little about it until Tryphena's death in 1890, at the beginning of the most sombre period of his life, when he remembered her as 'my lost prize'.

Work in Hicks's office was no more exacting than it had been during Hardy's pupillage, and he was more than five years away

*I read your name when you were strange to me,*
*Where it stood blazoned bold with many more;*
*I passed it vacantly, and did not see*
*Any great glory in the shape it wore.*

*O cruelty, the insight barred me then!*
*Why did I not possess me with its sound,*
*And in its cadence catch and catch again*
*Your nature's essence floating therearound?*

*Could* that *man be this I, unknowing you,*
*When now the knowing you is all of me,*
*And the old world of then is now a new,*
*And purpose no more what it used to be –*
*A thing of formal journeywork, but due*
*To springs that then were sealed up utterly?*

Mary Frances Scott-Siddons. Hardy saw her play Rosalind in *As You Like It* at the Haymarket Theatre on 20 April 1867 and wrote 'To an Actress' the following day

H. J. Moule's watercolour of Tincleton Heath: 'by Rushy Pond' is in Hardy's handwriting.

At Rushy-Pond

*On the frigid face of the heath-hemmed pond*
*There shaped the half-grown moon:*
*Winged whiffs from the north with a husky croon*
*Blew over and beyond.*

*And the wind flapped the moon in its float on the pool,*
*And stretched it to oval form;*
*Then corkscrewed it like a wriggling worm;*
*Then wanned it weariful.*

*And I cared not for conning the sky above*
*Where hung the substant thing,*
*For my thought was earthward sojourning*
*On the scene I had vision of.*

*Since there it was once, in a secret year,*
*I had called a woman to me*
*From across this water, ardently –*
*And practised to keep her near;*

*Till the last weak love-words had been said,*
*And ended was her time,*
*And blurred the bloomage of her prime,*
*And white the earlier red.*

*And the troubled orb in the pond's sad shine*
*Was her very wraith as scanned*
*When she withdrew thence, mirrored, and*
*Her days dropped out of mine.*

from it in experience. 'Almost suddenly he became more practical, and queried of himself definitely how to achieve some tangible results from his desultory yet strenuous labours at literature during the previous four years.' Moule suggested that he might combine architecture with a little reviewing, but this never interested Hardy. He later wrote one or two essays on literary matters and memoirs of George Meredith, Robert Louis Stevenson and William Barnes, but a review of the latter's *Poems of Rural Life in the Dorset Dialect* in 1879 was his only venture in criticism.

As things stood in 1867, Hardy's attempts to capture emotion in poetry had failed to excite any editor to the extent of a reasoned rejection. On the other hand, a simple unpretentious narrative called 'How I Built Myself a House', written primarily to amuse the pupils at Blomfield's, had been published by *Chambers's Journal* in 1865. Now he saw the most promising course in a novel, based on his knowledge of 'West-country life in its less explored recesses and the life of an isolated student cast upon the billows of London with no protection but his brains'.

'The Poor Man and the Lady' was never published, although it was cannibalised for later books and part of it recast for the story 'An Indiscretion in the Life of an Heiress'. In Hardy's words it was a 'sweeping dramatic satire of the squirearchy and nobility, London society, the vulgarity of the middle class, modern Christianity, church-restoration, and political and domestic morals in general, the author's views, in fact, being obviously those of a young man with a passion for reforming the world'. Some of the veiled passion of the previous five years went into the story. Hardy had seen several radical demonstrations in London and had longed to harangue the mob with the confidence shown in the novel's hero.

The drawing from Wessex Poems for 'Her Dilemma'

Her Dilemma
*(In —— Church)*

*The two were silent in a sunless church,*
*Whose mildewed walls, uneven paving-stones,*
*And wasted carvings passed antique research;*
*And nothing broke the clock's dull monotones.*

*Leaning against a wormy poppy-head,*
*So wan and worn that he could scarcely stand,*
*– For he was soon to die, – he softly said,*
*'Tell me you love me!' – holding long her hand.*

*She would have given a world to breathe 'yes' truly,*
*So much his life seemed hanging on her mind,*
*And hence she lied, her heart persuaded throughly*
*'Twas worth her soul to be a moment kind.*

*But the sad need thereof, his nearing death,*
*So mocked humanity that she shamed to prize*
*A world conditioned thus, or care for breath*
*Where Nature such dilemmas could devise.*

(*opposite*) Hardy's birthplace

(*overleaf*) The north Cornish Coast near St Juliot, the scene of Hardy's courtship of Emma Lavinia Gifford.

*The place is pre-eminently (for one person at least) the region of dream and mystery. The ghostly birds, the pall-like sea, the frothy wind, the eternal soliloquy of the waters, the bloom of dark purple cast that seems to exhale from the shoreward precipices, in themselves lend to the scene an atmosphere like the twilight of a night vision.*

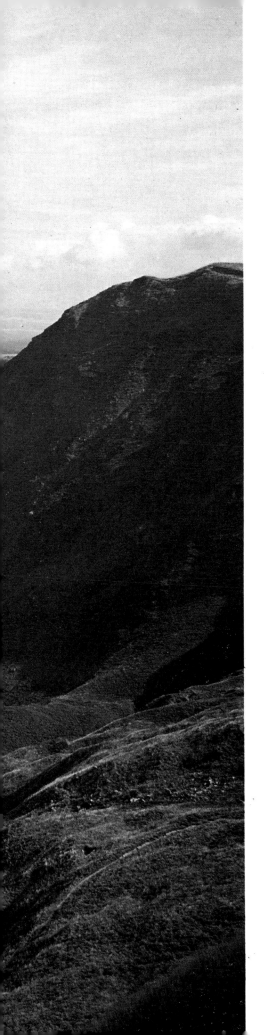

"When I set out for Lyonnesse"

When I set out for Lyonnesse,
A hundred miles away,
The rime was on the spray,
And starlight lit my lonesomeness
When I set out for Lyonnesse
A hundred miles away.

What would bechance at Lyonnesse
While I should sojourn there
No prophet durst declare,
Nor did the wisest wizard guess
What would bechance at Lyonnesse
While I should sojourn there.

When I came back from Lyonnesse
With magic in my eyes,
None managed to surmise
What meant my godlike gloriousness,
When I came back from Lyonnesse
With magic in my eyes.

T

On Stoureastle Foot-bridge

(1877.)

Reticulations creep upon the slack stream's face
When the wind skims irritably past,
The current clucks smartly into each hollow place
That years of flood have scrabbled in the pier's sodden base;
The ~~water~~ floating lily leaves rot fast.

On a roof stand the swallows equidistantly in rows,
Till they arrow off & drop like stones
Among the eyot-withies at whose roots the river flows;
And beneath the roof is she who in ~~a~~ the dark world shows
~~Like a white~~ as a lamp light when midnight moans.

Manuscript of the poem later revised and re-named 'On Sturminster Foot-bridge'.

(*opposite*) View from Riverside Villa, Sturminster Newton, showing the foot-bridge and boat house.

Another scene in a sunless church where the heroine, condemned by her caste to marry an equal, confesses that she loves none but the low-born hero, recalls 'Her Dilemma' (1866).

Like the reviewers of his first published novel *Desperate Remedies*, those who saw 'The Poor Man and the Lady' recognised Hardy's strengths and weaknesses immediately. They praised the naturalness and warmth of the rustic scenes and noted the descriptions of scenic and atmospheric effects but hesitated before the cold artifice – what John Morley called the 'queer cleverness and hard sarcasm' – of his handling of sophisticated society. What they had in fact discovered was that Hardy had no experience on which to base such scenes. He learned what was wanted of him very quickly and by the time of his third novel was striding firmly over his own ground, where he always remained at his best. When Hardy arranged his work for the Wessex Edition in 1912, the volumes were divided into 'Novels of Character and Environment' on the one hand and 'Romances and Fantasies' and 'Novels of Ingenuity' on the other. It is not coincidental that the division is that between his major and his minor fiction; between, for example, *The Mayor of Casterbridge* and *Tess of the d'Urbervilles* on the one hand, and *Desperate Remedies* and *A Laodicean* on the other.

'The Poor Man and the Lady' had been sent to Alexander Macmillan in July 1868. He and his reader Morley commented on it in detail: 'If this is your first book', they said, 'you ought to go on'. But Hardy, who had already conceded to necessity by turning from poetry to prose, wanted to get into print immediately. On Macmillan's advice that the novel might find a home in a house less fastidious than his, Hardy accepted his offer of an intro-

(*above*) Hardy saw the announcement of Meredith's death on a poster in London on 18 May 1909. He wrote 'George Meredith' in The Athenaeum immediately afterwards.

George Meredith
(1828–1909)

*Forty years back, when much had place*
*That since has perished out of mind,*
*I heard that voice and saw that face.*

*He spoke as one afoot will wind*
*A morning horn ere men awake;*
*His note was trenchant, turning kind.*

*He was of those whose wit can shake*
*And riddle to the very core*
*The counterfeits that Time will break....*

*Of late, when we two met once more,*
*The luminous countenance and rare*
*Shone just as forty years before.*

*So that, when now all tongues declare*
*His shape unseen by his green hill,*
*I scarce believe he sits not there.*

*No matter. Further and further still*
*Through the world's vaporous vitiate air*
*His words wing on – as live words will.*

(*left*) The Royal Parade, Weymouth in 1870. Hardy lodged at Weymouth intermittently in 1869–72.

duction to Frederic Chapman of Chapman & Hall. Chapman was tempted, but his reader, who turned out to be George Meredith, delivered Hardy a long lecture on the folly of putting his name to anything with so much purpose in it, if he wanted to have any future as a writer. If he wanted to catch the public eye, Meredith said, he should try something purely imaginative, on the lines of Chapman & Hall's most successful author Wilkie Collins.

Hardy went back to Dorset chastened but determined. In his spare time during the winter of 1868-9, with Meredith's sonorous words in his mind, he wrote *Desperate Remedies*. Many years later, after Hardy had seen the worn old man which Augustus John produced as a portrait of him, he had a dream in which he found himself carrying a heavy child, half Meredith and half John, up a ladder to safety: it was Meredith who turned Hardy into a publishable novelist and John who discerned how much the first half of his career took out of him.

When John Hicks died in 1868, his practice was taken over by the

Emma Lavinia Gifford (standing), with her sister Helen and the Rev. Caddell Holder at St Juliot, August 1870

St. Juliot Church 1870. (Before Restoration)
Showing transept & Nave (now North Aisle)
Thomas Hardy.

Weymouth architect G. R. Crickmay, who had no knowledge and less interest in the church-restoration work which formed a part of it. He asked Hardy to help with the completion of such contracts in that field as were in hand. One of them was at St Juliot in north Cornwall, where Hicks had been asked to act some years before. Hardy had been struck by the romantic name, but thought no more of it until one day early in 1870, when he was at Bockhampton trying to finish *Desperate Remedies*, Crickmay wrote to him suggesting that something ought to be done about it. Hardy refused, but Crickmay wrote again at the end of February asking him to go down and survey the church. Reluctantly, Hardy agreed.

The scattered parish of St Juliot lies around the River Vallency which enters the sea at Boscastle. In 1870 the rector was Caddell Holder, who ran the parish with the help of his second wife and her sister, Emma Lavinia Gifford, born on 24 November 1840. 'It was a difficult parish', wrote Emma in her *Recollections*, 'from neglect by a former incumbent.' The dilapidated church-tower 'went on cracking from year to year' and 'still the architect continued delaying to send his head man to begin operations'. Both Helen Holder and her sister worked hard, appealing to the patron to authorise work on the church and raising funds for it, in Emma's case by selling sketches.

(*below*) One of Emma Gifford's sketches of St Juliot church before restoration

The Giffords were not an easy family. Emma's father had been a solicitor in Plymouth but passed half his life with financial expectations which were not fulfilled when his mother died. Thereafter he drank. There was also present in the family a strain, if not exactly of insanity, then of rather awkward eccentricity, evident in Emma's thirtieth year in the childish delight she took in shocking the natives as she rode her horse recklessly at full speed along the Cornish cliffs. She was temperamentally quite unsuited to the eminently Victorian role of maiden aunt, and in any case the Holders had no children. They were anxious to marry her off to anyone who would have her and had almost come to an arrangement with a local farmer when Hardy appeared on the scene.

Hardy left Bockhampton soon after four in the morning on Monday, 7 March for the fifteen-hour journey to St Juliot. The railway took him as far as Launceston, whence there remained the 'dreary yet poetical drive' of sixteen miles to the rectory. The poetry of those three hours in the dry breeze of a fine March evening emerged in 'The Wind's Prophecy' and its answer 'A Man was Drawing Near to Me'; and the whole experience to which they led was encapsulated at the moment of infatuation by 'When I Set Out for

(*opposite*) Hardy at the time of his first visit to St Juliot

(*below*) Emma as she was when Hardy first met her. 'She Opened the Door' was written in 1913, after her death.

*She opened the door of the West to me,*
*With its loud sea-lashings,*
*And cliff-side clashings*
*Of waters rife with revelry.*

*She opened the door of Romance to me,*
*The door from a cell*
*I had known too well,*
*Too long, till then, and was fain to flee.*

*She opened the door of a Love to me,*
*That passed the wry*
*World-welters by*
*As far as the arching blue the lea.*

*She opens the door of the Past to me,*
*Its magic lights,*
*Its heavenly heights,*
*When forward little is to see!*

(*above*) Bench-ends at St Juliot destroyed during the church's restoration, drawn by Hardy in March 1870

Lyonnesse' and in the remorse of widowerhood forty-three years later by 'She Opened the Door'.

Bench Ends - St. Juliot Church - Cornwall -
1870.
T. Hardy. del.

'Received by young lady in brown,' Hardy noted of his arrival. Emma noticed his 'familiar appearance', 'slightly different accent' and the paper, a poem, sticking out of his pocket. Mr Holder had gout, so throughout his stay Hardy was much in Emma's company. The purpose of the visit seems to have been accomplished on its first day, which he spent at the church deciding how much of the ancient building would have to be demolished and making drawings, including some of the furniture which was later destroyed owing to the unsupervised zeal of the contractor. But Hardy stayed on until the end of the week, visiting Boscastle, Tintagel, the Penpethy slate quarries (to inspect material for the church roofing) and Beeny Cliff where, on a later visit, he sketched Emma against the forbidding scene. 'Scarcely any author and his wife', she wrote, 'could have had a much more romantic meeting... at this very remote spot, with a beautiful sea-coast, and the wild Atlantic Ocean rolling in with its magnificent waves and spray....'

Shortly after his return to Dorset, Hardy left to spend part of the summer 'desultorily and dreamily' in London. By the autumn, he regarded himself as 'virtually if not distinctly engaged to be married'. On his second visit in August he saw 'The Young Churchwarden' who had been the previous tenant of Emma's heart, and there

Beeny Cliff (Aug. 22. '70)

The Figure in the Scene.

....'I stood back that I might pencil it<br>
With her amid the scene;<br>
Till it gloomed & rained'.

(Moments of Vision.)

came a time when Hardy lamented that his chance arrival at St Juliot had ever led to his eviction. But for a while Emma fascinated him. She was the first woman he knew at all well who was not preoccupied with the basic struggle of life, unassailably genteel – she even had an uncle who was a canon of Worcester – and yet prepared to take an interest in him and his work. From Emma's side, Hardy was by far the most interesting man who had ever crossed her path. In spite of the slight vulgarity, the voice more attuned to the responses than the verses and the 'business appearance', he had a profession and hidden depths in his poetry. Yet the poison in the relationship, their fundamentally different attitudes to life, is apparent in the way each reacted to their meeting. In Emma's eyes, the chain of circumstances that led Hardy so far as St Juliot out of his normal courses showed that 'an Unseen Power of great benevolence directs my ways'. To Hardy, writing the poem 'Ditty' in the summer of 1870, it was further evidence of:

What bond-servants of Chance
We are all.

Alexander Macmillan refused to publish *Desperate Remedies*. Possibly in the fear of another lecture from Meredith instead of a contract, Hardy by-passed Chapman & Hall and sent it on to William Tinsley, then the leading publisher of popular fiction, who had declined 'The Poor Man and the Lady' with no comment beyond 'Return' scrawled across Hardy's letter inquiring about it. He agreed to take *Desperate Remedies* in return for a guarantee against loss of £75 – rather more than half Hardy's savings – and certain revisions, which Emma lovingly incorporated in the fair copy she made during the autumn.

''Pon my soul, Mr Hardy,' said Tinsley later, 'you wouldn't have got another man in London to print it! Oh, be hanged if you would! 'twas a blood-curdling story!' Nor would Hardy ever have written such a book but for the need 'to attract public attention at all hazards'. He had therefore contrived an amazing procession of incidents to lure on a readership saturated with great fiction and to raise their eyebrows by episodes like the pioneering lesbian scene between Miss Aldclyffe and Cytherea, the first of Hardy's flighty heroines. 'We tale-tellers', he wrote much later, 'are all Ancient Mariners, and none of us is warranted in stopping the Wedding Guests (in other words, the hurrying public) unless he has something more unusual to relate than the ordinary experience of every average man and woman.'

Nevertheless, most of what reviewers liked about *Desperate Remedies* had been drawn from the scene before him as he wrote rather than from his imagination: some of the Weymouth scenes, recalling the evenings when Hardy had rowed round the bay while he was working for Crickmay there; the topography of Stinsford, with the palatial Kingston Maurward House, its humbler predecessor nearby and the reminder of the transience of it all in the Grey monument in the church, which had fascinated him as a boy. There are also the local characters, the progenitors of the rustic choruses of later novels, and above all Edward Springrove drawn, according to Hardy, from an assistant who had come to Crickmay's office shortly after he started to write the novel, although the solid, self-effacing Springrove, who is further disregarded for social reasons and is 'a thorough bookworm – despises the pap-and-daisy school of verse – knows Shakespeare to the very dregs of the foot-notes. Indeed, he's a poet himself in a small way', must contain much of his creator.

John Morley had advised Macmillan not to touch *Desperate Remedies* because the story originated in the violation of a young lady. When it appeared anonymously in March 1871, few critics failed to notice this fact, nor to draw attention to the 'coarseness' and 'unpleasantness' of the whole thing. But all found some merit in the book and hoped to hear more of the author: 'We see no reason', said the *Athenaeum*, 'why he should not write novels only a little, if at all, inferior to the best of the present generation.' Horace Moule's comments in the *Saturday Review* were particularly understanding, but Hardy paid most attention to the *Spectator*'s hatchet job, in which John Hutton described the novel as a 'desperate remedy for an emaciated purse' (Hardy eventually lost £15 on it); and his suggestion that it was the work of an author who 'cannot do a better description of work, and must do some-

(*below left*) The monument of Audeley and Margaret Grey in Stinsford church. Hardy's gaze was often riveted on the skull during services in his childhood. Edward Springrove stood beneath it during Cytherea's marriage to Manston in *Desperate Remedies.*

(*below right*) The Temple overlooking the lake at Kingston Maurward, where Miss Aldclyffe persuaded Cytherea to marry Manston in *Desperate Remedies*

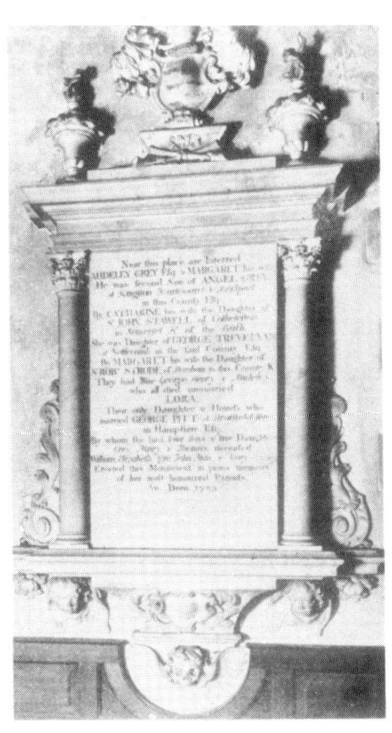

The Old Manor House, Kingston Maurward, was the seat of the Grey family until their last heiress Lora married George Pitt, who built the new house. Manston lived in part of it in *Desperate Remedies*.

thing' cut deepest of all into a failed poet. Nevertheless, Hardy had been launched, noticed and generally welcomed in a literary world still ruled by the work of Thackeray, Trollope, Dickens and George Eliot, and there was euphoria enough in that. He promptly sat down and wrote one of his best books.

(*opposite*) The keeper's cottage in Yalbury Wood, Geoffrey Day's house in *Under the Greenwood Tree*

(*inset opposite*) One of the Stinsford church-choir's music-books. The signature is that of Hardy's grandfather

One reason why *Under the Greenwood Tree* was written so quickly is because up to one-third of it, the scenes of the tranter's house, family and circle, were salvaged from 'The Poor Man and the Lady'. Another is that Hardy's enthusiasm for writing at last brimmed over, washing away all the encrusted advice he had been given and the inhibitions of his hard-won sophistication. 'You are original', Sir Leslie Stephen told him a little later, 'and can stand on your own legs.'

'The Mellstock Quire', the musicians who had played with Hardy's father and grandfather for forty years in the gallery of Stinsford church, formed the outer ring of his family circle during his childhood. As a poem like 'Friends Beyond' shows, he felt very close to them, and when as an old man he took visitors at Max Gate to inspect the graves in Stinsford churchyard the ones occupied by members of the choir were pointed out as carefully as those of his own family.

In the days when the splendours and complications of an organ were beyond the means of small parishes, church music was provided by an instrumental group consisting of a few strings and sometimes a little wind. The melancholy air of them, tuned a half-tone below modern pitch, winding their way through the immemorial melodies adapted to Tate and Brady's metrical psalms, moved Hardy as a child as much as the more fervent music of the dance. He once said that he would rather have been a cathedral organist than

(*below*) Hardy's drawing for 'Friends Beyond' in *Wessex Poems*. Hardy often communed with the dead in Stinsford churchyard and wrote several poems about them as well as 'Friends Beyond', including 'Paying Calls':

*I went by footpath and by stile*
*Beyond where bustle ends,*
*Strayed here a mile and there a mile*
*And called upon some friends.*

*On certain ones I had not seen*
*For years past did I call,*
*And then on others who had been*
*The oldest friends of all.*

*It was the time of midsummer*
*When they had used to roam;*
*But now, though tempting was the air,*
*I found them all at home.*

*I spoke to one and other of them*
*By mound and stone and tree*
*Of things we had done ere days were dim*
*But they spoke not to me.*

Each part did well In concert move
How brisk the time did beat
Our notes such melting strains of Love
that she cry'd out repeat
Our musick was so charming sweet
We play'd it three times o'er
But when I could No more repeat
She Laugh'd And cry'd Encore
Thomas Hardy

anything else in the world and he was always a willing servant of the power of music, which he used often in his novels and made the basis of one short story, 'The Fiddler of the Reels'.

The choir was the axis of village life. Hardy possessed his family's music-books in which sacred pieces were copied from the front and secular from the back, so that aberrations like the one described in 'Absentmindedness in a Parish Choir', when the band struck up 'The Devil among the Tailors' instead of Tallis's Canon, to Bishop Ken's Evening Hymn, were a genuine risk after a heavy night and a long sermon. The schoolmistress slaving over a harmonium or one strong arm manipulating a barrel organ (at Stinsford, it was that of Hardy's uncle James) tended to be more reliable, and in the rigorous religious climate that came on around 1850 the choirs soon disappeared. In Hardy's view, they took some of the cohesion of village life with them.

The tide of confidence on which *Under the Greenwood Tree* was written turned before the autumn when Hardy received an ambiguous letter from Alexander Macmillan which he interpreted as another refusal. Throwing the manuscript aside in disgust, he went back to London and architecture. There the future was darkened further by a deterioration in his eyesight which might eventually have ruined him as a draughtsman; and this possibility, along with his faith in Hardy's abilities, caused Moule to encourage him not to give up writing altogether.

Love was not the consolation it might have been, for Hardy was not getting the kind of obsessive attention he wanted from Emma. 'Love the Monopolist' suggests that they reacted to the sensation in different ways. When they were apart, Hardy would sink into love-sick gloom:

> 'O do not chat with others there,'
> I brood. 'They are not I.
> O strain your thoughts as if they were
> Gold bands between us; eye
> All neighbour scenes as so much blankness
> Till I again am by!

While for Emma love infused life as a whole:

> While with strained vision I watch on,
> The figure turns round quite
> To greet friends gaily; then is gone....

Hardy's complaint was not quite fair and Emma, albeit aided by a lack of opportunity, was by far the more constant of them during the four and a half years between their meeting and their marriage. During this time Hardy visited Emma six or seven times in

Helen Paterson, the illustrator of *Far from the Madding Crowd*

Cornwall and once in Bath, where she was staying with friends of her family, and in between saw a lot of Annie Thackeray, Leslie Stephen's sister-in-law. He also formed an active liking for Helen Paterson, the illustrator of *Far from the Madding Crowd*, who shortly afterwards married the novelist William Allingham.

One day while Hardy was walking in the Strand Tinsley, who had just remaindered *Desperate Remedies*, came up and asked him for another novel. Hardy asked his parents to look for the manuscript of *Under the Greenwood Tree* and in due course sold it to Tinsley for £30. Although it was well reviewed and noticed in some very influential circles which were to bear fruit later on, Hardy's second novel was not a success. Tinsley tried very hard to sell it and issued illustrated and paperback editions, but *Under the Greenwood Tree* was too pure and too short to rouse any interest. Still, he liked Hardy's writing and decided to set him to work ploughing the richest field in Victorian fiction with a twelve-part serial for his magazine.

From *A Pair of Blue Eyes* onwards all Hardy's novels first appeared as serials in magazines before being published in book form. The

magazines, like Smith, Elder's *Cornhill* and Chatto & Windus's *Belgravia,* had been founded during the 1850s by book publishers to show their authors in a tempting form. Publication in a small edition of two or three expensive and hard-wearing volumes aimed mainly at the commercial circulating libraries followed and then, if a novel was a major success, a single cheap book. The magazines had enormous circulations, whose tastes and prejudices had to be carefully observed, and several of Hardy's novels had to be clipped in flight in order to sit comfortably in the Grundian nest. Hardy quietly deplored that he had ever sunk to practise as a 'good hand at a serial' but he was grateful, especially to the *Cornhill*, whose jubilee in 1910 he celebrated with a poem.

For his first serial Hardy asked Tinsley for twice what he could hope to earn at architecture in nine months and, although not much of it was planned and still less written, Tinsley agreed immediately. He wanted the first instalment almost at once, and in those days when, as Hardy told Sir Sydney Cockerell many years later, he was writing 'from hand to mouth' he finished it in a few frenzied nights before leaving for Cornwall by boat from London Bridge at the beginning of August 1872.

Hardy always liked to be close to what he was writing about, and Cornwall is the scene of *A Pair of Blue Eyes*. 'The place', he wrote in a preface to a later edition of the novel,

> is pre-eminently (for one person at least) the region of dream and mystery. The ghostly birds, the pall-like sea, the frothy wind, the eternal soliloquy of the waters, the bloom of dark purple cast that seems to exhale from the shoreward precipices, in themselves lend to the scene an atmosphere like the twilight of a night vision.

The setting and the companionship of Emma helped him to write a story which, although full of regularly spaced sensations to satisfy the magazine readers, was characteristic enough of Hardy's best to draw a letter from Coventry Patmore acclaiming it as 'more poetry than prose'. The suggestion by later inquirers that the novel was strongly autobiographical gave Hardy no pleasure at all, but he drew heavily enough on some aspects of what had passed between Emma and himself to make it necessary to disguise the topography in earlier editions and generally to avoid upsetting a family as prickly as the Giffords by the portrayal of one of their number in the pages of a vulgar periodical.

Hardy had been introduced to Emma's father John Gifford during the summer and directed some of the proofs of *A Pair of Blue Eyes* to be sent to him at Kirland, Gifford's house near Bodmin, while he was staying there in September. By this stage in his life Gifford was incapable of being less than disgruntled about anything, and his reception of Hardy as a prospective son-in-law was not warm.

(*opposite above*) Lanhydrock House, near Bodmin, from which 'Endelstow House' in *A Pair of Blue Eyes* was drawn

(*opposite below*) Kirland House, near Bodmin, rented by Emma Gifford's parents

But there were no material advantages dependent on his approval,

*of Blue Eyes* as it developed. From
great deal about his mind and the nature of his imagination, at work in scenes which she may have suggested indirectly from what she told him about her own life. How, for example, as a child at Plymouth she had slipped over a cliff and hung on by a tuft of grass until rescued. Hardy used a scene like it in the novel but not for mere dramatic effect, for as Knight clings to the rock, face to face with a fossil, in chapter 32 Hardy ran through his mind a complete essay on the oneness of creation and the vanity of man.

She told him also about her previous admirers. According to 'The Face at the Casement' one of them was dying, and with infuriating open-heartedness she insisted on going to see him while Hardy was down there. If this suggested the story of Felix Jethway in the novel, Emma would have seen that it was not the simple pathos of the case that Hardy relied on but the imagined vengeance of Jethway's mother. His unerringly baleful eye was to cause her real distress later on but, if she realised what she was in for, she was blinded by infatuation and her sister's encouragement, and married Hardy as soon as it was practicable to do so.

While Hardy was finishing *A Pair of Blue Eyes* at Bockhampton in December 1872, he received a letter addressed in 'a hand so fine that it might have been traced with a pin's point'. He was lucky to get it because the arm of civilisation, as represented by postal deliveries, reached out to Bockhampton rather infrequently in the 1870s and the children entrusted with carrying the letter from Dorchester had dropped it in the mud on the way, whence it was rescued by a labourer. It was from Leslie Stephen, who had succeeded Thackeray as editor of the *Cornhill Magazine* the previous year. Moule had told him that Hardy was the author of *Under the Greenwood Tree*, and Stephen was impressed by it. 'It is long', he said, 'since I have received more pleasure from a new writer and if you are, as I hope, writing anything more, I should be very glad to have the offer of it for our pages.'

Stephen was a more muscular version of Horace Moule and after the latter's death had a greater influence on Hardy's thinking than any other contemporary. He had been born into the inner circle of the intellectual aristocracy and despatched along a familiar road by way of Eton to Holy Orders and a Cambridge fellowship. But he became an untameable rationalist and eventually left the Church, choosing Hardy to witness his deed renouncing Holy Orders. While Stephen was militantly agnostic, Hardy was far too interested

Leslie Stephen.
Among his other achievements, Stephen was an accomplished mountaineer and the first man to climb the Schreckhorn in the Swiss Alps. Hardy saw the mountain during a visit to Switzerland in 1897: 'Then and there I suddenly had a vivid sense of him, as if his personality informed the mountain – gaunt and difficult like himself. As I lay awake that night, the more I thought of the mountain, the more permeated with him it seemed: I could not help remarking to my wife that I felt as if the Schreckhorn were Stephen in person; and I was moved to begin a sonnet to express the fancy.'

The Schreckhorn
*(With thoughts of Leslie Stephen)*
(June 1897)

*Aloof, as if a thing of mood and whim;*
*Now that its spare and desolate figure gleams*
*Upon my nearing vision, less it seems*
*A looming Alp-height than a guise of him*
*Who scaled its horn with ventured life and limb,*
*Drawn on by vague imaginings, maybe,*
*Of semblance to his personality*
*In its quaint glooms, keen lights, and rugged trim.*

*At his last change, when Life's dull coils unwind,*
*Will he, in old love, hitherward escape,*
*And the eternal essence of his mind*
*Enter this silent adamantine shape,*
*And his low voicing haunt its slipping snows*
*When dawn that calls the climber dyes them rose?*

in the self-evident power of the supernatural and unexplained over

Christmas Eve for any reason other than [illegible]
it might be so'. He did share the agnostics' perspective of Christianity: 'We enter church and we have to sing "My soul doth Magnify the Lord", when what we want to sing is "O that my soul could find some Lord that it could magnify". Till it can, let us magnify good works, and develop all means of easing mortals' progress through a world not worthy of them.'

When he asked him to write the serial that eventually became *Far from the Madding Crowd,* Stephen knew nothing of *A Pair of Blue Eyes* in which Hardy had mastered the basic principles of serial writing. It was with *Under the Greenwood Tree* in mind that Stephen emphasised the need not for 'a murder in every number' but 'to catch the attention of readers by some distinct and well-arranged plot'. Stephen's problems turned out to be quite different, for he had come to Hardy's side at the moment when he was ready to start sailing through the winds of taste rather than with them. Quite soon, Stephen's powerful personality and ruthless standards – his approval, Hardy once said, was 'disapproval minimised' – became almost oppressive to him, but at the time of *Far from the Madding Crowd* he was resolute enough. 'We stood shoulder to shoulder against the British public', Hardy told Stephen's daughter Virginia Woolf in 1926, 'about certain matters dealt with in that novel.'

By the time Hardy started to plan *Far from the Madding Crowd* he realised that the novel would not be his last and that, as a writer who had been noticed mainly for his evocation of the countryside, his exceptionally retentive visual memory was going to be far too important to him to be confined to the facts of an earthbound territory. Like Trollope before him, for quite different reasons, he decided to fictionalise his ground. The name 'Wessex', which first appeared in chapter 50 of *Far from the Madding Crowd,* was originally intended to represent little more than Dorset itself but grew to include two-thirds of southern England. Hardy did not altogether succeed in achieving the freedom of description he wanted. Charting the topography of his novels rather soon became something of a cult and brought ranks of pertinacious inquirers to his doors. To please them, he drew a map of the limited setting of *The Return of the Native* and went to some trouble to standardise the terrain in the first collected edition of his work in the 1890s. The associated pedantries seem to have given him little pleasure although scope for some gentle mockery of them: 'I once spent several hours on a bicycle with a friend in a serious attempt to discover the real spot', he wrote in a preface to *The Woodlanders* about the imaginary site of Little

Woodbury Hill Fair.
*Greenhill was the Nijni Novgorod of South Wessex; and the busiest, merriest, noisiest day of the whole statute number was the day of the sheep fair.*
*(Far from the Madding Crowd)*
This was Hardy's first use of the name 'Wessex'. 'Greenhill' was his name for Woodbury Hill

Hintock, 'but the search ended in failure; although tourists assure

Hardy's Wessex, Hardy told him: 'I have no objection to it whatever – if you print somewhere on the map (or in any text

(*left*) Hardy's map for *The Return*

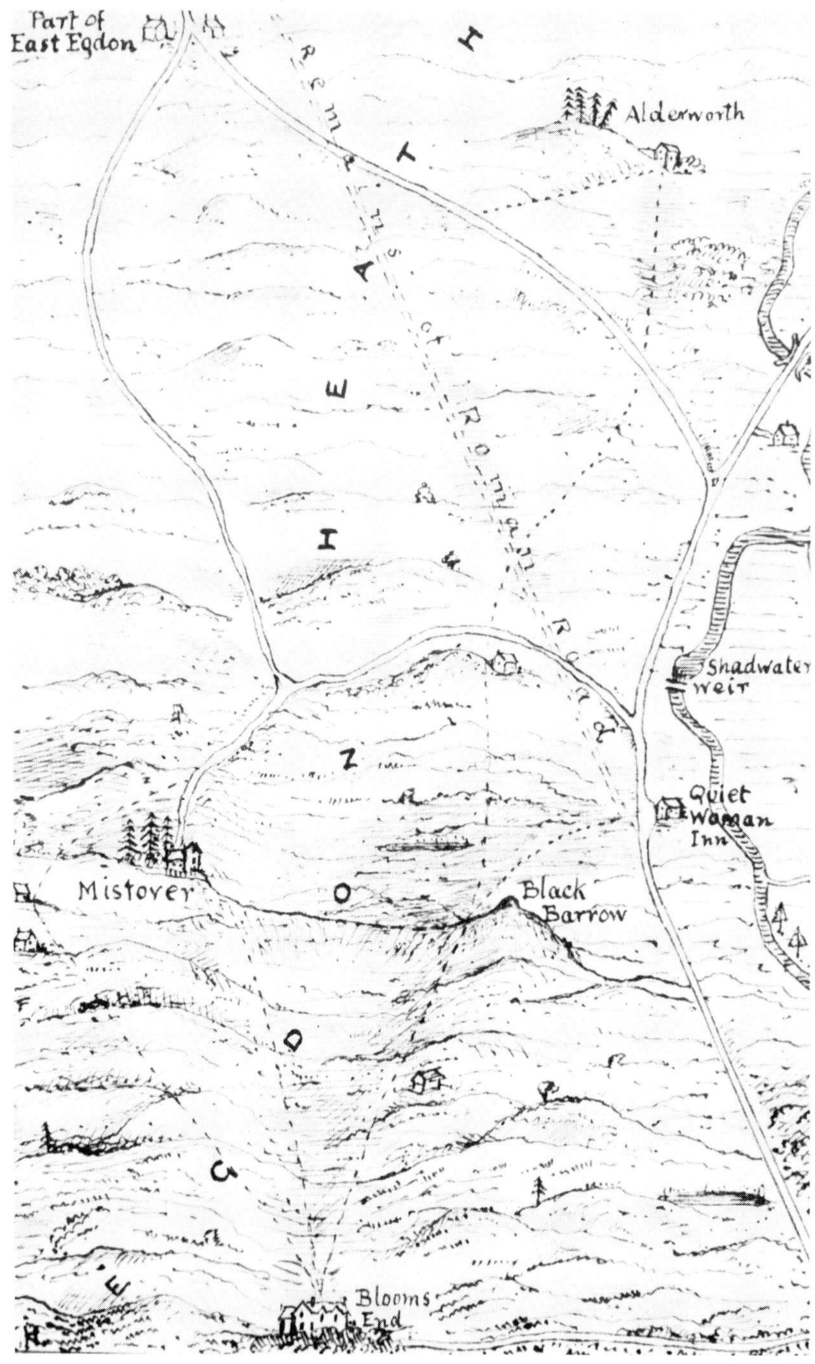


(*opposite*) The country of *The Trumpet-Major*.

(*opposite*) Countryside near Cerne Abbas.

accompanying it) that the places in the novels were only *suggested* by those real ones given – as they are not literally portraits of such.' Similarly, one of his very rare public speeches, on receiving the Freedom of Dorchester in 1910, was largely devoted to saying that 'Casterbridge' is *not* Dorchester. There were other disadvantages, which he pointed out in another letter to Lea: 'In case you should be thinking of giving a view of spots in Bockhampton as scenes in *Under the Greenwood Tree* ( or any other purpose), I think I ought to let you know that there are reasons against it – not the least being the nuisance occasioned to those who live there by trippers with Kodaks looking over the hedges, and other undesirable visitors,

Puddletown, the 'Weatherbury' of Wessex

which would be increased by the publication of such views.'

... to provide a

recognised it. They ...
were among the most deprived in the country, or that the union activist Joseph Arch was particularly busy among them, still less that Hardy had heard Arch speak at a hiring fair in February 1873 while he was writing the novel. Such was not yet his purpose. But when, many years later, his secretary suggested that the country around Stinsford must have been a 'Gray's *Elegy* sort of place', he replied immediately: 'Stinsford *is* Stoke Poges.' A few years before he wrote *Far from the Madding Crowd*, Hardy had reflected that 'the most prosaic man's life becomes a poem when you stand by his grave and think of him'. In the novel he set out to show that the inhabitants of timeless rural communities were led only by circumstance to 'blush unseen' and could show extremes of strength and folly worthy of major figures on the stage of history.

Hardy knew his types extremely well, from the priceless worth of a conscientious shepherd like Immanuel Riggs of Puddletown, who died in 1872 and on whom he probably based Gabriel Oak, to the

(*below*) The sheep-washing pool at 'Weatherbury Upper Farm'.
*'To birds on the wing its glassy surface, reflecting the light sky, must have been visible for miles around as a glistening Cyclops' eye in a green face.'*

(*opposite*) A Dorset shepherd

feckless dregs of society who drank their way apologetically through life. He knew too, and described with unconcealed venom, the type of Sergeant Troy, who debauched their leisure hours from barracks in Dorchester flashing about amid the ferns in the surrounding country and making the most of Fanny Robin and her kind.

Stephen's readers wanted neither an idyll nor a melodrama, but some of the plainer aspects of Hardy's account of rural life were not to their liking either. After a few instalments of *Far from the Madding Crowd* had appeared in the *Cornhill* early in 1874, Stephen began to get letters questioning the direction which the story of Fanny Robin was taking: '. . . excuse this wretched shred of concession to popular stupidity', he wrote to Hardy, but 'may I suggest that Troy's seduction of the young woman will require to be treated in a very gingerly fashion, when, as I suppose must be the case, he comes to be exposed to his wife? I mean that the thing must be stated but that the words must be careful.' So when the moment

Lulworth Cove.
*He undressed and plunged in. Inside the cove the water was uninteresting to a swimmer, being smooth as a pond, and to get a little of the ocean swell Troy presently swam between the two projecting spurs of rock which formed the pillars of Hercules to this miniature Mediterranean. Unfortunately for Troy a current unknown to him existed outside, which, unimportant to craft of any burden, was awkward for a swimmer who might be taken in it unawares. Troy found himself carried to the left and then round in a swoop out to sea.*

came for Troy to be unmasked, Bathsheba's servant Liddy 'came close to her mistress and whispered in her ear' and the *Cornhill's* readers, having assumed the worst, read on with their pinces-nez undisturbed.

Within the novel Hardy would have felt closest to Bathsheba and Boldwood, the small landowners isolated by their responsibilities and comparative wealth as he now was from his father's circle by his learning and vocation. His solitude was deeper than theirs, for as he sat writing day after day under the thatch at Bockhampton the only sympathetic ear within reach was his mother's; and, while she was a fund of information, she was no judge of an advanced piece of fiction. Hardy's most valued props were all more than a hundred miles away. Emma was told very little about it. For a while he still had Moule to lean on when he chose; but in September 1873, when *Far from the Madding Crowd* was one-third written. Moule cut his throat in his rooms at Cambridge.

Moule's academic difficulties had not been the only problem in his life. Prostitutes were prominent among his father's flock in Fordington. Horace had patronised and had a child by one of them. According to his brother Charles, giving evidence at the inquest, Horace had 'suffered for some time past from exceeding depression of mind... extreme beyond any adequate cause'. The exact cause of Moule's melancholia was unmentionable at the time and unprovable now. 'Standing by the Mantelpiece' suggests that Hardy knew it and somehow felt responsible for launching the chain of events which led to the suicide. Moule's act of self-destruction lowered over the remaining pages of *Far from the Madding Crowd* and marked a step in the development of Hardy's view that there was someting fundamentally perverse about any supernatural power that could

Waterston House, the model for Bathsheba Everdene's 'bower'

One of the gargoyles at Stinsford church. For the purposes of *Far from the Madding Crowd* Hardy transferred it to Puddletown.
*It was too human to be called like a dragon, too impish to be like a man, too animal to be like a fiend, and not enough like a bird to be called a griffin. This horrible stone entity was fashioned as if covered with a wrinkled hide; it had short, erect ears, eyes starting from their sockets, and its fingers and hands were seizing the corners of its mouth, which they thus seemed to pull open to give free passage to the water it vomited . . . . the creature had for four hundred years laughed at the surrounding landscape, voicelessly in dry weather, and in wet with a gurgling and snorting sound.*

countenance such things.

'If *Far from the Madding Crowd* is not written by George Eliot', wrote a reviewer of the still-anonymous first instalment of the serial version, 'then there is a new light among novelists.' With it, Hardy stepped into the front rank of living novelists and remained there as long as he chose to write prose fiction. Before the end of 1874 *Far from the Madding Crowd* had been reprinted seven times. Its success was anticipated by that of the serial, and Hardy seemed assured of an income from a source at which he was willing to persevere and the means on which to marry. He married Emma at St Peter's Church, Paddington, on 17 September 1874. Canon Gifford, who shortly afterwards became Archdeacon of London, came up from Worcester to perform the ceremony, but apart from Emma's brother Walter, who gave her away, no other members of either family were present. The circumstances and place of the wedding, after so long a courtship, suggest that all was not as it might have been. Hardy evidently appreciated Canon Gifford's gesture of goodwill, and the only known presentation copy of *Far from the Madding Crowd* was given to him.

After a few days on the south coast, the honeymoon was spent in France, first at Rouen, where Hardy would have lectured Emma with Ruskin in his hand, and then in Paris. Neither of them had been abroad before. Emma kept a charmingly impressionistic diary of all they saw: 'the Louvre', she noted, 'is very French'.

For more than ten years the Hardys had no permanent home. On their return from France they moved into the first of a succession of rented rooms and houses in London and Dorset, where for three or four years they had few possessions apart from Hardy's boxes of books which followed them, sometimes in store and sometimes strewn around the lodging-house floor.

'All romance ends at marriage,' Hardy had written in *Far from the Madding Crowd,* and so it seems to have been. After years of yearning for requited love, Hardy recoiled from the facts of cohabitation. Before their marriage he can have spent no more than three months with Emma and very little of that alone with her. Emma's exuberance and buoyancy, so captivating in small doses on the Cornish cliffs, very soon became a strain on Hardy exposed to her day after day in a few small rooms. Hardy could never bear to be touched and he now found himself positively enbosomed by a vigorous and demanding woman whom he was at a loss to satisfy. On a wet afternoon in Bournemouth in July 1875, when they were looking for a place where he could write another novel, irritation began to break through:

> We were irked by the scene, by our own selves; yes,
> For I did not know, nor did she infer
> How much there was to read and guess
> By her in me, and to see and crown
> By me in her.

West End Cottage, Swanage, where the Hardys spent the winter of 1875–6

Poole Harbour, c. 1880

As a witch-flame's weirdsome sheen
At the minute of an incantation scene;
And it greened our gaze — that night at ~~plenilune~~ demilune.

Roaring high & roaring low was the sea
Behind the headland shores:
It ~~mocked~~ symbolled the slamming of doors,
Or a regiment ~~treading~~ hurrying over hollow floors....
And there we two stood, hands clasped; I & she!

St Aldhelm's Head

They settled for the winter of 1875-76 in Swanage, in the house of an invalided merchant sea-captain. Bockhampton had been close enough to the south coast for Hardy to know something of the sea, and he relished this opportunity to learn more from his garrulous landlord's reminiscences and smuggling stories. He regularly crossed the harbour to Poole, to chat to other sailors there and gather material for stories like 'To Please his Wife'. In the other direction, he led Emma on excursions along the shore and cliffs to Durlstone Head and on to within sight of St Aldhelm's. They were humbled by the grandeur of nature around them, but some of the poems of the time, like 'To a Sea-Cliff' and 'Once at Swanage', suggest the beginnings of jealousy in Emma's attitude and in Hardy a dread of the future.

Hardy had been flattered but not pleased by the comparison of *Far from the Madding Crowd* with the work of George Eliot, whom he always admired more as a thinker than as a creative writer, and that is one reason why *The Hand of Ethelberta* was quite unlike it. He put aside the woodland story he had in mind and wrote instead a social comedy, one of the 'Novels of Ingenuity' at which he never shone. Henry Holt, Hardy's first American publisher, had questioned the wisdom of following *A Pair of Blue Eyes* so quickly with *Far from the Madding Crowd*: 'Probably no one but Shakespeare', he said, 'has ever been able to accomplish the best class of work with any rapidity.' Hardy did actually write fairly quickly, and most of his novels were set down within a year. They had to be, because very often his manuscript would be only one or two instalments ahead of what was already in print in serial form. But he did like time to plan and sometimes research the background of his novels before he began to write. Until the last ten years of his career as a novelist, when he was writing with a purpose and with more accumulated material to hand than he could use, pot boilers alternated pretty regularly with his best. Both Stephen and Hardy had no doubt that *The Hand of Ethelberta* was one of the former. Even Emma did not like it much – 'too much about servants in it'.

The interlude between *The Hand of Ethelberta* and *The Return of the Native* was not long but it was a period of unequalled tranquillity in Hardy's life, which he came to look back on as an 'idyll'. In June 1876 he rented a house overlooking the Stour at Sturminster Newton. Riverside Villa was the first home that they had to themselves, and they spent the happiest years of their marriage there. Emma was able to enlarge her personality as the mistress of a modest house in the receptive community of a small town, and Hardy to enjoy the Blackmore Vale, 'this fertile and sheltered tract of country where the fields are never brown and the springs never dry', and to explore the prehistoric forts, Hod, Hambledon and

(*opposite*) Corfe Castle, the 'Corvsgate Castle' of *The Hand of Ethelberta*

(*right*) The mill, Sturminster Newton

(*below*) Riverside Villa, Sturminster Newton. The Monkey Puzzle, which Hardy planted in the autumn of 1876, was felled in 1962

… the chalk ridge along the horizon. The Stour

through the reeds on summer …
addressing the piers of the foot-bridge.

But the smiling land, like the inconstant sky over Hardy's native heath, was a deception. At Sturminster, where nature was at its most lavish and even their servant became pregnant, Emma remained childless and the distance between them unbridged. 'Your novel', she had told him while he was writing *Far from the Madding Crowd*, 'seems sometimes like a child, all your own and none of me'; and, as Hardy's style developed, his work became ever more his exclusive interest.

Hardy was now confident enough in his powers to be concerned to protect his style: to look at nature's defects full in the face and find in them 'the basis of a hitherto unperceived beauty'. Leslie Stephen very early noticed what T. S. Eliot later described as Hardy's inability to leave anything to nature and his insistence

Holland's Farm, Tincleton – Diggory Venn's 'fifty-cow dairy'. The bearded figure is Hermann Lea.

H. J. Moule's watercolour of Rainbarrow.
*This bossy projection of earth above its natural level occupied the loftiest ground of the loneliest height that the heath contained. Although from the vale it appeared but as a wart on an Atlantean brow, its actual bulk was great. It formed the pole and axis of this heathery world.*

on giving 'one last turn of the screw himself'. One of Stephen's excisions from *Far from the Madding Crowd* had been Bathsheba's view of Fanny Robin's child in her coffin – 'with a face so delicately small in contour and substance that its cheeks and the plump backs of its little fists irresistibly reminded her, excited as she was, of the soft convexity of mushrooms on a dewy morning' – and it had trodden too heavily on what Hardy called his 'idiosyncratic mode of regard'.

Stephen did not ask for a serial to follow *The Hand of Ethelberta* and Hardy was wary of exposing *The Return of the Native* to his surveillance. Hardy tried, unsuccessfully, to sell it elsewhere before showing the first seven chapters to him in August 1877. Stephen was impressed but feared that 'the relations between Eustacia, Wildeve, and Thomasin might develop into something "dangerous" for a family magazine', so there Hardy's association with the *Cornhill* ended. The editor of *Belgravia*, which started to publish the serial a few months later, was not so intrusive, although he did insist on some relief to Hardy's meticulously worked-out five-act tragedy by the addition of a sixth book containing a happy ending.

*The Return of the Native* was conceived as a purely pastoral story. Hardy set it in the harsh country behind his birthplace, where the bliss of maggots wriggling in the mire could be looked at favourably beside the lot of its human inhabitants struggling to tame the 'imperturbable countenance of the heath, which, having defied the cataclysmal onsets of centuries, reduced to insignificance by its seamed and antique features the wildest turmoil of a single man'. Hardy's evocation of the moods and beauty of the heath has

most celebrated piece of prose. He could, no doubt, have

monochrome the precious

Other writers might have set the whole saga of mismating and frustrated ambition in the confessional, but Hardy needed a lurid theatrical background. Even so, some of the reviewers implied that the author of *The Return of the Native* was out of touch: 'People talk', said one, 'as no people ever talked before.' Hardy had decided before this that, to sustain him through the grind of serial writing, it would be useful if he lived in London and moved a little in the literary circles where he could now be welcome. In March 1878, when two-thirds of *The Return of the Native* were written, the Hardys' gave up Riverside Villa and moved to Tooting.

(*opposite*) The country of *The Woodlanders. It was one of those*

*grandeur and unity ... enacted . . . .*

Hardy never really liked London. He had a horror of lying down in the company of 'a monster whose body had four million heads and eight million eyes', but even after his three years at Tooting he continued to spend a few months there in most years until he was over eighty. In later years, when Emma frequently remained alone in Dorset, the justification for the annual upheaval was that he thoroughly enjoyed being exhibited in fashionable society. The circles

Shadwater Weir, where Eustacia Vye and Damon Wildeve were drowned in *The Return of the Native*, and where Retty Priddle tried to drown herself in *Tess of the d'Urbervilles*.
In his youth, Hardy watched the recovery of a body from the pool. From that incident, *The Return of the Native* developed.

(*right*) Edmund Gosse

he was drawn into in 1878 were rather more bohemian and not to Emma's taste at all. Hardy did not exactly scintillate in them either. His shyness remained unconquered and after the jolliest evenings his fellow guests would go away feeling, like William Dean Howells, that 'after all I had only shaken hands with Hardy across the threshold'. Rather less kindly, Edward Marsh recalled Hardy as 'content to bask in Gosse's beams, and I never heard him say anything that couldn't have been said by the most self-effacing parasite'.

Edmund Gosse was one of the permanent and valued friends whom Hardy made in London in the late seventies. He was then emerging as a critic and by the turn of the century had grown to take the place of some of the eminences of the previous generation like Matthew Arnold and Leslie Stephen. He had a gift for the perilous path of friendship between public criticism and private comment and was to be a particular support to Hardy against the obloquy that followed *Jude the Obscure*. When they first met, Gosse was acting as the London adviser of some of the American publishers who were interested in Hardy's work, and working for

(*opposite*) The Frome Valley

the main & upper decks. They [illegible]

short, & they put the short men below.

Bob, though not tall, was not likely to be specially selected for shortness. She pictured him on the upper ~~upper~~ ~~main~~ deck, in his snow-white trousers & jacket of navy blue, looking perhaps towards the very point of land where she then was.

The great silent ship, with her population of blue jackets, marines, officers captain, & the admiral who was not to return alive, passed like a phantom the meridian of the Bill. Sometimes her aspect was that of a large white ~~grey~~ bat, sometimes that of a grey one. In the course of time the watching girl saw ~~fancied~~ that the ship had passed ~~was withdrawing~~ her nearest point; & saw the breadth of her sails diminished by foreshortening, till she assumed the form of an egg on end. After this something seemed to twinkle, & Anne, who had previously withdrawn from the old sailor, went back to him, ~~again~~ & looked again through the glass. The twinkling was the light falling upon the cabin-windows of the ship's stern. She explained it to the old man.

"Then we see now what the enemy have seen but once. That was in seventy-nine, when she sighted the French & Spanish fleet off Scilly, & she retreated because she feared a landing. Well, 'tis a brave ship, & she carries brave men!" ~~[illegible]~~ [Anne's tender bosom heaved; but she said nothing, & again became absorbed in contemplation: ~~the~~] ~~& Anne again took a few steps westward~~. The Victory was fast dropping away.

~~She murmured in a voice of sweet solemnity: They that go down to the sea in ships, that do business in great waters; these see the works of the Lord & his wonders in the deep.~~

She ~~The Victory~~ was on the horizon, & soon appeared hull down. That seemed to be ~~like the beginning of the end~~ a greater end than her present vanishing. Anne Garland ~~She~~ could not stay by the sailor any longer, & went about a stone's throw off, where she was hidden by the inequality of the cliff from his view. The vessel was now exactly end on, & stood out in the direction of the Start, her width having contracted to the proportion of a

(*above*) Robert Browning

(*opposite*) A page from the manuscript of chapter 34 of *The Trumpet-Major,* in which Anne Garland watches the *Victory* sail past Portland Bill on her way to Trafalgar

(*below*) Hardy's drawing for 'The Alarm' in *Wessex Poems,* showing his grandfather on the Ridgeway between Dorchester and Weymouth, looking towards Portland

a reform of the international copyright laws and an end to the pirated editions of popular authors which kept Hardy a comparatively poor man until his last years.

By degrees, Hardy 'fell into line as a London man'. He joined the Savile Club which, until he passed on to the communal solitude of the Athenaeum, he used often, and frequented dining clubs like Sir Walter Besant's 'declaration for virility in literature', the Rabelais Club. In Hardy's view, not all its members were notable for the virility of their style. They included Henry James, 'who has a ponderously warm manner of saying nothing in infinite sentences'.

One of the *salons* which Hardy was pressed into attending was that of Mrs Anne Benson Procter, who persistently maintained that Henry James wanted to marry her, although he was forty years her junior. Mrs Procter's role seems to have been somewhat passive. 'She sat', Hardy recalled, 'in a fixed attitude, almost as if placed in her seat like an unconscious image of Buddha' but around her fawned some like Browning, who had been the acolytes of his literary odyssey.

The dedication of Browning's narrative poem *Sordello* – 'incidents in the development of a soul: little else is worth study' – could equally be the motto of substantial collections of Hardy's poetry. He had worshipped Browning when he himself began to write seriously in the 1860s. When Hardy got to know him at Mrs Procter's and elsewhere he sometimes envied Browning's unique position as a popular poet and an advanced thinker, and questioned how he

'Th[illegible] I live' he wrote to Gosse in 1899,

of a [illegible]
vast a seer and feeler when on neutral ground! . . . [illegible] had a theory which you will call horrible – that perceiving he would obtain in a stupid nation no hearing as a poet if he gave himself in his entirety, he professed a certain mass of commonplace opinion as a bait to get the rest of him taken.

In 1875-8 the Napoleonic era was particularly on Hardy's mind. During those years he wrote the poems 'Valenciennes', 'The Alarm', 'San Sebastian', 'Leipzig', 'The Sergeant's Song', part of which was used in *The Trumpet-Major*, as well as the story 'A Tradition of Eighteen Hundred and Four'.

During Hardy's childhood the years 1803-5 were still the most vividly remembered years in the lives of the oldest surviving generation who, like his grandmother, were in their garrulous dotage and wont to reminisce about them at length. The countryside, too, was full of casual relics of the time:

Sutton Poyntz, the 'Overcombe' of *The Trumpet-Major*

> An outhouse door riddled with bullet holes, which had been extemporized by a solitary man as a target for firelock practice when the landing was hourly expected, a heap of bricks and clods on a beacon-hill, which had formed the chimney and walls of the hut occupied by the beacon-keeper, worm-eaten shafts and iron heads of pikes for the use of those who had no better weapons, ridges on the down thrown up during the encampment, fragments of volunteer uniform, and other such lingering remains, brought to my mind in early childhood the state of affairs at the date of the war more vividly than volumes of history could have done.

Although he thought about writing at least one other, *The Trumpet-Major* is Hardy's only historical novel, and he went to considerable trouble with his material. Much of the time during his first year at Tooting, after he had finished *The Return of the Native,* was spent at the British Museum, taking exhaustive notes from 'volumes of history' on the period, especially the naval and military practice of the time and George III's sojourns at Weymouth when he had taken time off from the waters to review the yeomanry encamped on the downs. Most of it found a place in the novel, but more was absorbed by Hardy's reconstruction of the alarm from private knowledge. He must have been tempted to make more of the character of his putative kinsman Captain Hardy, but he put it aside for later use on a larger canvas. Hardy was far too conscious of the shadow of Thackeray's *Vanity Fair* to say all he wanted to say about the Napoleonic era in a novel, and let it rest as a good read.

While Hardy was writing *The Trumpet-Major,* the American owners of *Harper's New Monthly Magazine* decided to launch a European edition. They wanted the most popular authors and offered extremely attractive terms. In Hardy's case this was £100 for each of twelve instalments. His price was still modest by comparison with some, like George Eliot who had been paid £7000 for *Romola* twenty years before. The first instalment of *A Laodicean* was scheduled to appear in December 1880, and Hardy began to feel increasingly ill while he was writing it during the early autumn. In October he suffered an internal haemorrhage and took to his bed. The doctor suggested either a hazardous operation or a long period of complete immobility, where he would have to lie for much of the time with his feet at a higher level than his head. Hardy was not yet tired enough of life to risk the operation and chose instead five months of constant intimacy with Emma.

If he had had no obligations to meet, the output of Hardy the egocentric poet, trussed up and helpless in a sunless room in a dreary suburb, might have been vastly enriched by these months.

Tomb of John Beaufort, Duke of Somerset and his wife Margaret, in Wimborne Minster

## Copying Architecture in an Old Minster
*(Wimborne)*

*How smartly the quarters of the hour march by*
*That the jack-o'-clock never forgets;*
*Ding-dong; and before I have traced a cusp's eye,*
*Or got the true twist of the ogee over,*
*A double ding-dong ricochetts.*

*Just so did he clang here before I came,*
*And so will he clang when I'm gone*
*Through the Minster's cavernous hollows – the same*
*Tale of hours never more to be will he deliver*
*To the speechless midnight and dawn!*

*I grow to conceive it a call to ghosts,*
*Whose mould lies below and around.*
*Yes; the next 'Come, come,' draws them out from their posts,*
*And they gather, and one shade appears, and another,*
*As the eve-damps creep from the ground.*

*See – a Courtenay stands by his quatre-foiled tomb,*
*And a Duke and his Duchess near;*
*And one Sir Edmund in columned gloom,*
*And a Saxon king by the presbytery chamber;*
*And shapes unknown in the rear.*

*Maybe they have met for a parle on some plan*
*To better ail-stricken mankind;*
*I catch their cheepings, though thinner than*
*The overhead creak of a passenger's pinion*
*When leaving land behind.*

*Or perhaps they speak to the yet unborn,*
*And caution them not to come*
*To a world so ancient and trouble-torn,*
*Of foiled intents, vain lovingkindness,*
*And ardours chilled and numb.*

*They waste to fog as I stir and stand,*
*And move from the arched recess,*
*And pick up the drawing that slipped from my hand,*
*And feel for the pencil I dropped in the cranny*
*In a moment's forgetfulness.*

As it was, while he made up his mind to return to poetry as soon as he could possibly do so, such strength as he had was given to feeding *Harper's* each month with 12,500 words of an unremarkable novel. For Emma, it was an exceptional opportunity to re-enter his life but she did not succeed. From the poem 'Beyond the Last Lamp', written in 1879, it is clear that Hardy had given up hope that marriage might lighten the burden of his life:

> The pair seemed lovers, yet absorbed
> In mental scenes no longer orbed
> By love's young rays. Each countenance
> As it slowly, as it sadly
> Caught the lamplight's yellow glance,
> Held in suspense a misery
> At things which had been or might be.

After two difficult years, during which Emma had slavishly fulfilled at least one of her marriage vows, she was put in her place by a passage in the preface to *A Laodicean:*

> As some of these novels of Wessex life address themselves more especially to readers into whose souls the iron has entered, and whose years have less pleasure in them now than heretofore, so 'A Laodicean' may perhaps help to while away an idle afternoon of the comfortable ones whose lines have fallen to them in pleasant places: above all, of that large and happy section of the reading

(*below*) The White Horse Inn, Maiden Newton, before it was rebuilt in 1900.
It was the scene of part of Hardy's first short story 'Destiny and a Blue Cloak'

not yet reached ripeness of years; those to

Things were easier in

quiet years, broken by visits to Scotland and Paris, from June 1881. As in Sturminster Newton, Emma found local society comparatively sympathetic, especially now that they had moved up to dining with the county court judge and the minor gentry. Of Dorset's three surviving monastic churches, Wimborne is the most mixed architecturally, with details representing all styles from the first Saxon building to a rather drastic restoration completed twenty-five years before the Hardys arrived. Hardy had just joined the newly founded Society for the Protection of Ancient Buildings, for whom he later wrote a paper on his 'Memories of Church Restoration', and spent some time in Wimborne Minster copying the bits that had survived Wyatt and communicating with the Beauforts and Courtenays buried there.

During his last months in Wimborne Hardy wrote his longest short story, 'Our Exploits at West Poley' which, like several of his other stories, was intended for children. His career as a short-story writer had begun in the autumn of 1874, when he wrote 'Destiny and a Blue Cloak' for the *New York Times*. He had no special regard for the short story as a literary form, although he wrote forty-seven in all, ranging from anecdotes to novelettes. His own favourite among them was 'The Son's Veto', a bitter account of the power of snobbery over natural affection, and made lighter use of a similar theme in 'A Tragedy of Two Ambitions'.

A substantial proportion of the stories reflect Hardy's strong and not too discriminating taste for the bizarre, gruesome and ironic. Instances of the unusual in any form were the staple of local journalism and gossip, and Hardy noted with care instances that appealed to him. Some that were not disinterred for use in his novels became the bases of stories. Davies, the Dorchester hangman, was an old friend of the Hardy family and a fund of usable incident, and one aspect of his services together with the most dramatic of folk remedies, the 'turn in the blood', was described in 'The Withered Arm'. Another story, 'An Imaginative Woman', turned on a current sensation in popular genetics, while 'On the Western Circuit' was a very quirky manifestation of Hardy's notion of idealised love.

Soon after they arrived in Wimborne Hardy started to plan his next novel, *Two on a Tower*. His conception of it was more ambitious than the finished work. He wanted to make astronomy 'not the padding of a romance, but the actual vehicle of romance'. He set about mastering the technical background with characteristic

(*right*) Hangman's cottage, Dorchester.
*At this date, and for several years after, there was a hangman to almost every jail . . . the Casterbridge official dwelt in a lonely cottage by a deep slow river flowing under the cliff on which the prison buildings were situate ('The Withered Arm')*

(*below*) 'T. Voss used to take casts of heads of executed convicts . . . there was a groove where the rope went' (Hardy's note, September 1888)

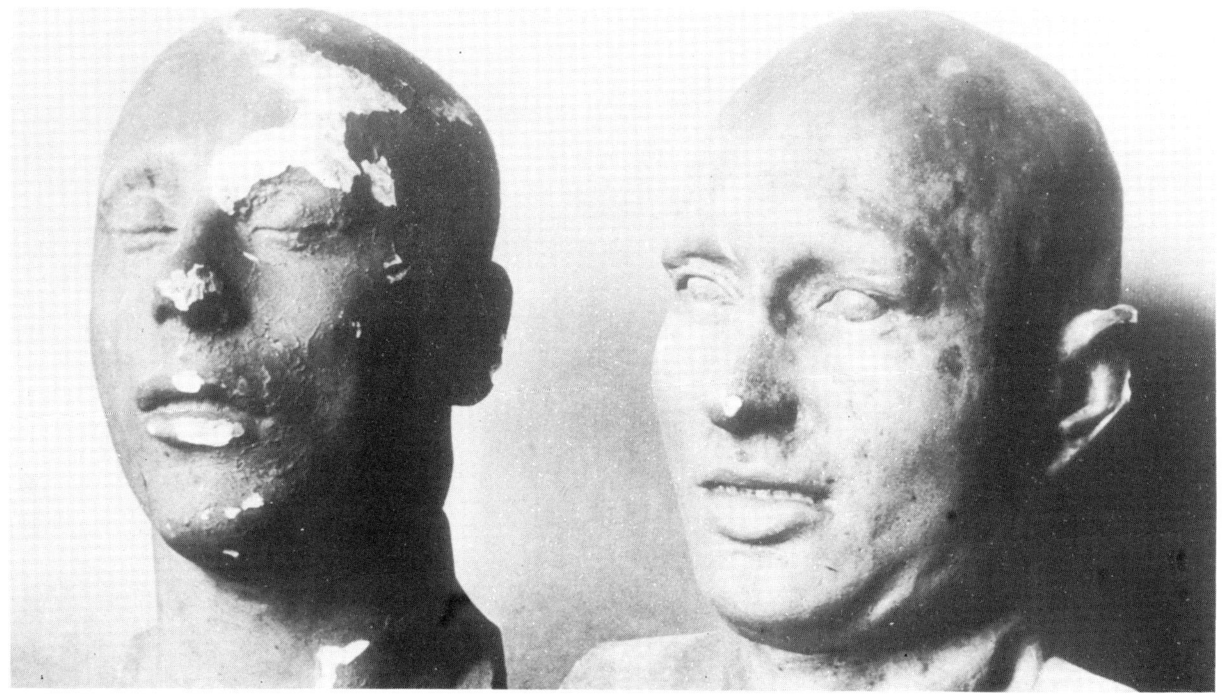

At a Lunar Eclipse

*Thy shadow, Earth, from Pole to Central Sea,*
*Now steals along upon the Moon's meek shine*
*In even monochrome and curving line*
*Of imperturbable serenity.*

*How shall I link such sun-cast symmetry*
*With the torn troubled form I know as thine,*
*That profile, placid as a brow divine,*
*With continents of moil and misery?*

*And can immense Mortality but throw*
*So small a shade, and Heaven's high human scheme*
*Be hemmed within the coasts yon arc implies?*

*Is such the stellar gauge of earthly show,*
*Nation at war with nation, brains that teem,*
*Heroes, and women fairer than the skies?*

thoroughness. By the autumn of 1881 he was corresponding with the astronomer W. C. Unwin about telescopes and lenses, and had been allowed to inspect the Royal Observatory at Greenwich, having assured the Astronomer Royal that he had no astrological purpose. Hardy sometimes wished that he had made *Two on a Tower* a more substantial work but, as he admitted to Gosse a few years later, 'though the plan of the story was carefully thought out, the actual writing was lamentably hurried. . . . It would have been rewritten for the book form if I had not played truant and gone off to Paris.'

The theme of the novel was an old one in his mind and constantly present in different guises in his work. The moon was Hardy's symbol for reality at its steeliest. In 'A Cathedral Façade at Midnight', for example, the pellucid certainty of the moon's beam creeping across the sculptured pomps of inherited belief seemed to draw

. . . sighings of regret
At the ancient faith's rejection
Under the sure, unhasting, steady stress
Of Reason's movement, making meaningless
The coded creeds of old-time godliness.

And in 'Shut out that Moon' she appears as one of nature's deceits, illuminating the happinesses of life doomed to decay:

Close up the casement, draw the blind,
Shut out that stealing moon,
She wears too much the guise she wore
Before our lutes were strewn
With years-deep dust, and names we read
On a white stone were hewn.

In *Two on a Tower,* his purpose was to 'set the emotional history of two infinitesimal lives against the stupendous background of the stellar universe, and to impart to readers the sentiment that of these contrasting magnitudes the smaller might be the greater to them as men'.

When Hardy lost his faith in the 1860s, he turned in search of an explanation of the meaning of existence to the scientific materialists who dominated the thinking of the later nineteenth century. He had been 'among the earliest acclaimers' of *The Origin of Species* and, however unsatisfactory its reasoning became to him, he retained enough respect for Darwin to attend his funeral in April 1882. Thinking in the light of Darwin set aside the consoling Christian expedient that every human being has a soul precious in the eyes of God and replaced it with stark alternatives: either the first cause of existence was unknown and unknowable, or the universe was a

life had appeared by

but for Hardy, to whom the hearts and
the most important things in life, they would not do. If men were nothing, it was intolerable that they should be capable of feeling and suffering, and still more that they should shackle one another by the morality and conventions of a discredited creed. Between them, these two ideas darkened his remaining work.

The obelisk on Weatherbury Castle, which suggested the site of 'Ring's-Hill Speer' for *Two on a Tower*

The Hardys' next move, in June 1883, was planned to be their last before settling somewhere permanently. Although their new lodging was in Dorchester, a small dark house near the gaol, it was not agreed that they would settle in the town or even in Dorset at all. Some of Hardy's new friends, Lord and Lady Portsmouth, offered to find them a house in Devonshire. Emma might have been pleased to return to her native county but by the autumn Hardy had bought an acre and a half of land from the Duchy of Cornwall just east of Dorchester. It was on the Wareham road, near the cottage of a former toll-gate keeper called Mack, and building work to Hardy's design began almost immediately.

For the time being Hardy was happy to be back in Dorchester. Durnovaria had been one of the first Roman cities in southern England: it 'announced old Rome in every street, alley and precinct. It looked Roman, bespoke the art of Rome, concealed dead men of Rome,' Hardy wrote of it in *The Mayor of Casterbridge*, and he threw himself into discovering its past, recent and remote. He seems to have read nearly every back number of the *Dorset County Chronicle and Somersetshire Gazette*, and not a few of the incidents in his subsequent novels can be traced to reports of events which he found there. He belonged to the Dorset Natural History and Antiquarian Field Club, to which he once read a paper; took a close interest in the Museum, then under the curatorship of Henry Moule, and shortly afterwards saw its present building rise in High West Street to the designs of his old master Crickmay.

Hardy's knowledge of Dorset's more remote past was based on the four volumes of the third edition of John Hutchins's *History and Antiquities of the County of Dorset*. It was a mine of fact and fantasy. 'The pedigrees of our county families,' he wrote in the preface to his collection of slightly shocking stories *A Group of Noble Dames* published in 1891, which he imagined members of the Field Club telling one another on a wet afternoon, 'arranged in diagrams on the pages of county histories, mostly appear at first sight to be as barren of any touch of nature as a table of logarithms. But given a clue – the

The bricked-up arch in the wall of Colliton House, Dorchester. It has been moved and re-erected in the Dorset County Museum.
*Originally the mask had exhibited a comic leer, as could still be discerned; but generations of Casterbridge boys had thrown stones at the mask, aiming at its open mouth; and the blows thereon had chipped off the lips and jaws as if they had been eaten away by disease.* (*The Mayor of Casterbridge*)

faintest tradition of what went on behind the scenes, and this dryness as of dust may be transformed into a palpitating drama.' Hardy soon became highly practised at communicating with the shades. The story of one of his 'Noble Dames', 'The First Countess of Wessex', came uncomfortably close to the facts of the career of the progenitress of the Fox-Strangways earls of Ilchester; and another, 'Barbara of the House of Grebe', which he presented as a simple and nasty gothic melodrama, was founded on the life of Barbara Webb, wife of the fifth Earl of Shaftesbury.

Then, in another context, there was the droll story of Sir

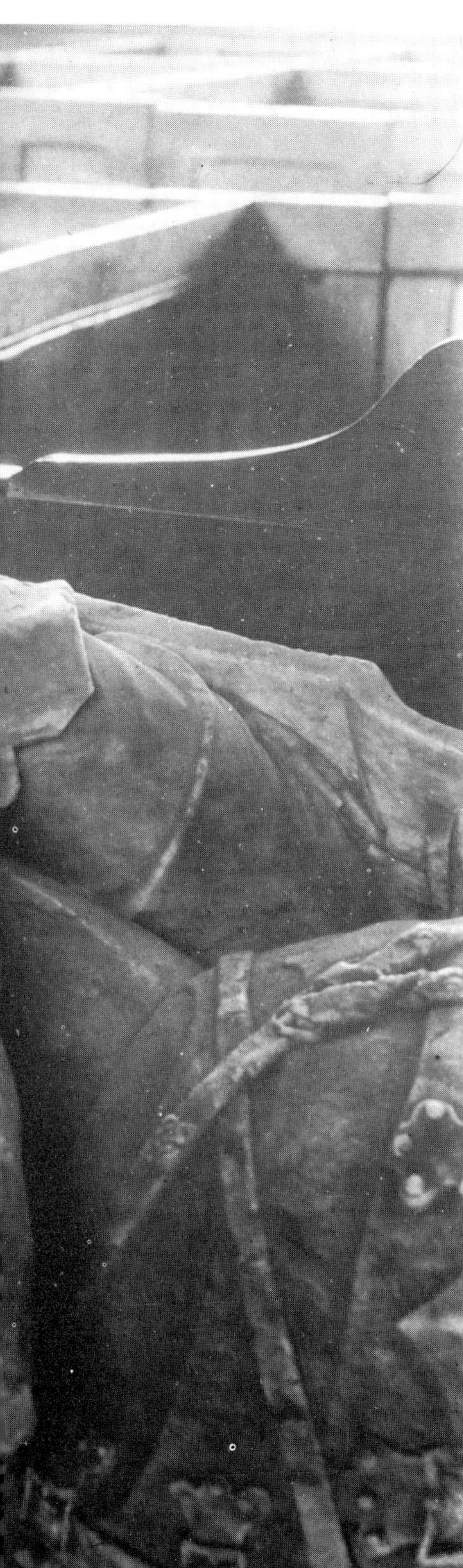

The Children and Sir Nameless

*Sir Nameless, once of Athelhall, declared:*
*'These wretched children romping in my park*
*Trample the herbage till the soil is bared,*
*And yap and yell from early morn till dark!*
*Go keep them harnessed to their set routines:*
*Thank God I've none to hasten my decay;*
*For green remembrance there are better means*
*Than offspring, who but wish their sires away.'*

*Sir Nameless of that mansion said anon:*
*'To be perpetuate for my mightiness*
*Sculpture must image me when I am gone.'*
*– He forthwith summoned carvers there express*
*To shape a figure stretching seven-odd feet*
*(For he was tall) in alabaster stone,*
*With shield, and crest, and casque, and sword complete:*
*When done a statelier work was never known.*

*Three hundred years hied; Church-restorers came,*
*And, no one of his lineage being traced,*
*They thought an effigy so large in frame*
*Best fitted for the floor. There it was placed,*
*Under the seats for schoolchildren. And they*
*Kicked out his name, and hobnailed off his nose;*
*And, as they yawn through sermon-time, they say,*
*'Who was this old stone man beneath our toes?'*

Effigy of Sir William Martyn, the builder of Athelhampton, in Puddletown church

(*left*) Melbury House, seat of the

William Martyn, the builder of Athelhampton, who so disliked children that he devoted all his procreative energy to the making of an alabaster effigy of himself in Puddletown church, which ended up as the foot-stool of village urchins.

History often moved more ethereal sentiments in Hardy. When the contractor's men were moving earth from Conquer Barrow to make the drive at Max Gate, they decapitated a complete family of Romano-British skeletons, two of which lay together like lovers in the same capsule in the chalk. For the purpose of his poem 'The Clasped Skeletons', Hardy pre-dated the remains by two thousand years, to set their continuing intimacy in the longest perspective of celebrated lovers, from Paris and Helena to Abelard and Héloïse:

So long, beyond chronology,
  Lovers in death as 'twere,
So long in placid dignity
    Have you lain here!

Yet what is length of time? But dream!
  Once breathed this atmosphere
Those fossils near you, met the gleam
    Of day as you did here;

But so far earlier theirs beside
  Your life-span and career,
That they might style of yestertide
    Your coming here!

Best of all Hardy liked history with a broad topographical base. He inspected every inch of Maiden Castle, the massive prehistoric fortress south of Dorchester, and described it in his story about the demented venality of an antiquary, 'A Tryst at an Ancient Earthwork'.

(*right*) Maiden Castle

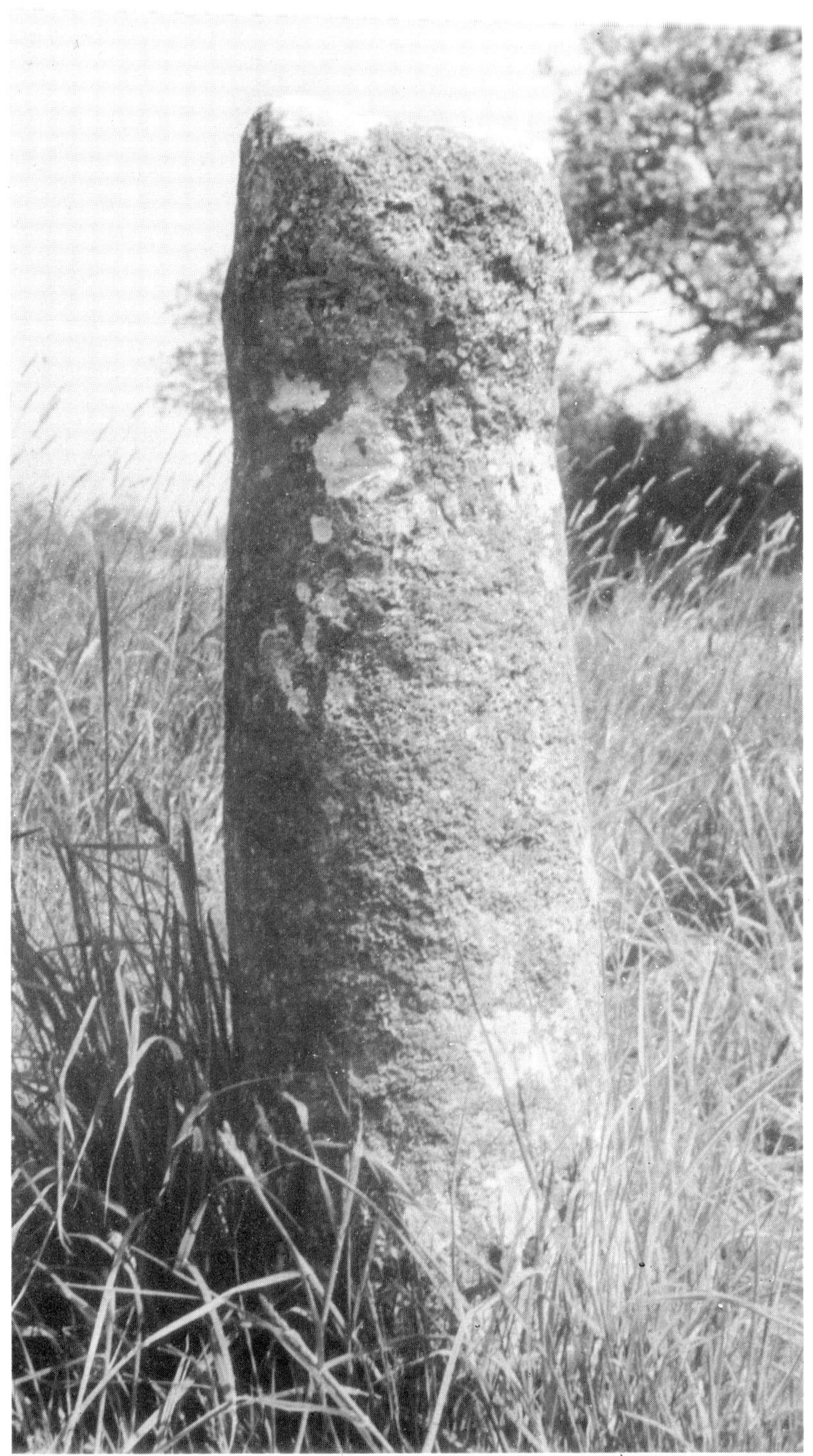

(*left*) Cross-in-Hand,
Batcombe Hill.
Alec d'Urberville made Tess swear on it that she would never wilfully tempt him again. Later, a shepherd told her: *'Cross – no; 'twer not a cross! 'tis a thing of ill-omen, Miss. It was put up in wuld times by the relations of a malefactor who was tortured there by nailing his hand to a post and afterwards hung. The bones lie underneath. They say he sold his soul to the devil, and that he walks at times.'*
Another version of the cross's meaning is related in 'The Lost Pyx'

The gatehouse, Cerne Abbey

Emma was never a good walker, but on a bicycle she became as agile as Hardy, and the vision of her bloomers as she free-wheeled down High East Street became a regular feature of Dorchester life. Hardy himself remained awheel until he was over eighty and in earlier years covered prodigious distances. One of his favourite landmarks was Cross-in-Hand, the stone pillar on Batcombe Hill, marking the 'site of a miracle, or murder, or both', which appears in *Tess of the d'Urbervilles*. The legend behind the cross told in 'The Lost Pyx' is the pious version, about the monk from Cerne Abbey who dropped the sacrament in the grass one night on his way to visit a dying man and found it surrounded by kneeling animals on a spot marked by a shaft of light from the sky. But Hardy knew the variants and some of the supplementary detail, like that recounted by Henry Moule:

> 'The priest was much astounded at what he saw, yet not so much so but that he observed among the live-stock a black horse, kneeling, indeed, like the rest, but only on one knee. The priest said to this lukewarm beast, 'Why don't you kneel on both knees, like the rest?' 'Wouldn't kneel at all if I could help it.' 'Who, then, are you?' 'The devil.' 'Why do you take the form of a horse?' 'So that men may steal me, and get hung, and I get hold of them. Got three or four already.'

While he was living in Dorchester, Hardy considered writing a novel set in the town in Roman times but turned instead to the Dorchester of his schooldays. *The Mayor of Casterbridge* has, nevertheless, a historical purpose. One of the first general themes in Hardy's work to be defined by critics was that of his own essay 'The Dorsetshire Labourer': the decline of traditional agricultural communities in the face of new requirements and new methods. 'The home Corn Trade,' he wrote in the preface, 'on which so much of the action turns, had an importance that can hardly be realized by those accustomed to the sixpenny loaf of the present date, and to the present indifference of the public to harvest weather.' The Corn Law agitation had been part of the general ferment during Hardy's childhood. At the age of six, he had rushed around the garden at Bockhampton brandishing a small wooden sword gored in a freshly slaughtered pig, yelling 'Free Trade or Blood!' The need to compete with cheap imported corn hastened the ruin of the likes of Michael Henchard, dependent in his corn-factoring business on weather prophets and mental arithmetic and further disabled by his intemperate character, and quickened the inexorable triumph of a new order, represented by the wiry Presbyterian Farfrae with his book-keeping and modern machinery.

Some of the scenes in *The Mayor of Casterbridge*, such as Henchard's bankruptcy proceedings, were drawn

and the availability

the nineteenth century. Skimmington rides, public demonstrations of disapproval of the conduct of married people, had been outlawed in 1882 but one was put on in a Dorset village as recently as 1917 and several were reported in 1884 when Hardy was writing the novel. Stories of men who, like Henchard, swore to abjure drink for specified terms of years were part of the basic rhetoric of self-help.

The writing of *The Mayor of Casterbridge* was unusually leisurely,

(*above right*) West end of the South Walks, Dorchester, in 1859, about

(*below right*) King's Arms, Dorchester.
The hotel appears in five of Hardy's novels, most conspicuously as the scene of Henchard's banquet in *The Mayor of Casterbridge*

KINGS ARMS
KINGS ARMS HOTEL

(*above*) Grey's Bridge, Dorchester, where Henchard and the other '*misérables* . . . of a politer stamp . . . bankrupts, hypochondriacs . . . shabby-genteel men' lounged away their time

and several months passed between its completion in April 1885 and the beginning of serial publication. Hardy made many alterations before it appeared in book form but did not soften its harsh conclusion or the message summarised by Henchard's step-daughter Elizabeth-Jane that in life 'happiness was but an occasional episode in the general drama of pain'.

Before the Hardys moved into Max Gate in June 1885, they planted several hundred Austrian pines in the grounds as a windbreak. They very quickly provided more seclusion as well, but as Max Gate was designed specifically to serve Hardy's solitary and well-ordered needs it is a curious house. While Dorchester remains one of the most compact towns in England, even in the 1880s Max Gate was within sight of one of the new suburbs and within sound of the railway. From the outside the building is a fairly commonplace, front-heavy, redbrick Victorian villa, although inside the four main rooms, which until the pines grew would have had a fine view south towards Came Down, are all completely different without being in the least fussy and generally very successful. Hardy made much of the hall and staircase in the space left after he had fitted in the dining-room and drawing-room on either side. But there was no library for his growing collection of carefully used books; and for a study he moved through a succession of rooms on the first floor, the last of which,

(*opposite*) Max Gate

(*left*) The drawing-room at Max

(*below right*) The hall and front staircase at Max Gate. The barometer had belonged to William Barnes

facing west, was part of a later extension over the kitchen. The other rooms, which never included a bathroom or lavatory in Hardy's lifetime, were fitted in where there happened to be gaps. Towards the end of her life Emma lived in obstinate seclusion in an attic, whence her comings and goings must have been very perilous indeed.

In their early days there Hardy sometimes wondered whether the expense of building Max Gate had been worth while. But once he felt that the house had absorbed the personalities of Emma and himself he became very fond of it and liked to think of their spirits being apparent to later inhabitants. Hardy was abnormally interested in psychic phenomena but always sceptical about their manifestations. He once said that he would give ten years of his life to see a ghost.

another novel. It was fifteen years since he had had any dealings with Macmillan, although the Hardys had seen something socially of Alexander Macmillan and his wife, especially during their years at Tooting. The firm was now run by Alexander's nephew Frederick and in July 1884, when Hardy was still at work on *The Mayor of Casterbridge,* the editor of his magazine had written to ask for a serial.

Hardy decided to return to the woodland story which he had put aside for *The Hand of Ethelberta* in 1874. By November 1885, he was hard at it: 'Have gone back to my original plot for *The Woodlanders* after all. Am working from half-past ten A.M. to twelve P.M., to get my mind made up on the details.' When he finished the novel

Hardy in his study at Max Gate, *c.*1904

Turnworth House, now demolished. Its setting suggested that of 'Hintock House': *To describe it as standing in a hollow would not express the situation of the manor-house; it stood in a hole. But the hole was full of beauty.*

eighteen months later he was relieved rather than pleased, although, next to *Far from the Madding Crowd, The Woodlanders* became his own favourite among his novels. For a setting he chose the hidden hamlets above the south-west corner of Blackmore Vale, a part of Dorset which he liked very much but had never described at length before:

> It was one of those sequestered spots outside the gates of the world where may usually be found more meditation than action, and more listlessness than meditation; where reasoning proceeds on narrow premisses, and results in inferences wildly imaginative; yet where, from time to time, dramas of a grandeur and unity truly Sophoclean are enacted in the real, by virtue of the concentrated passions and closely-knit interdependence of the lives therein.

(*left*) Part of the ruins of Sherborne

(*opposite*) View from the Cupola of the Sheldonian Theatre, Oxford. *It had windows all round, from which an outlook over the whole town and its edifices could be gained. Jude's eyes swept all the views in succession, meditatively, mournfully, yet sturdily. Those buildings and their associations and privileges were not for him.*

(*below*) Hurdle-making, one of Giles Winterborne's woodland pursuits in *The Woodlanders*

Max Gate, from the side garden.

In *The Woodlanders* Hardy carried his lifelong complaint about the cruelty of existence into its last phase. First he had railed against the cosmos, then denounced the avoidable frailties of men, now he began to quarrel with society. When Grace Melbury, a country girl rendered unfit for either simple or sophisticated life by the fashionable education lavished upon her by an ambitious parent, ponders her disastrous and indissoluble marriage to the philandering dilettante Fitzpiers, she neither curses Fate nor bewails the consequence of her lust and ambition. Instead, she asks herself calmly whether she is really joined in marriage by God or by Act of Parliament.

Hardy's reverence for architecture, painting and Classical literature led him at last to Italy in March 1887. Emma and he left for a month's visit immediately after he had finished *The Woodlanders*. Hardy's first glimpse of the 'Epic-Famed, god-haunted, Central Sea' from above Genoa was marred by the fishwives' lines of gaudy washing, but the journey as a whole was an infinitely satisfying pilgrimage. In Rome he felt almost oppressed by the weight of history around him. In the faces in the streets he saw 'Satyrs: Emperors: Faustinas', just as he detected the debased features of Digbys, Binghams and Turbervilles in the ordinary people of Dorchester.

As a practitioner at different levels in three of the arts and an informed observer of a fourth, Hardy was sensitive to most of the Muses. Under the marbled gaze of all nine, in the Sala delle Muse in the Vatican, he questioned his inconstancy but was reassured by his conviction that all the arts were one. He gave this answer in a poem, 'The Vatican: Sala delle Muse', when his poetry began to be published in the 1890s and critics, setting aside the facts of his career, accused him of abandoning his true vocation as a writer of prose.

Of all poets, Hardy would most have liked to meet Shelley who, like his near rival in Hardy's heart Keats, died in Italy and was buried in the Protestant Cemetery at Rome in the shade of the pyramid of the otherwise unknown Cestius. All Hardy's work is steeped in the writing of others, sometimes in formal quotation and sometimes subsumed by the flow of his own. Next to Shakespeare and the Bible, Shelley and Keats appear more than any others. When he was asked to name the finest passage in poetry, Hardy chose stanzas 85–7 from Canto III of Byron's *Childe Harold* but he regarded Shelley as 'our most marvellous lyrist' and the line 'O World! O Life! O Time!' from 'A Lament' as the best single poetic expression. Shelley's spirit permeates the Chorus of the Pities in *The Dynasts*, just as Keats's 'Ode to Sorrow', quoted on the title-page of *The Return of the Native*, is all but the novel's motto.

On his return from Italy in April, Hardy found *The Woodlanders* acclaimed in a way in which none of his novels had been since

(*left*) Milton Abbey.

first Earl of Dorchester ... mansion to the north of the Abbey and was irked by the proximity of the village. He bought in the leases, demolished the houses and moved such of the inhabitants as clung to the soil to a 'model' village built for the purpose half a mile to the south-east. Hardy related part of the story in 'The Doctor's Legend'.

Rome
The Vatican: Sala delle Muse
(1887)

*I sat in the Muses' Hall at the mid of the day,*
*And it seemed to grow still, and the people to pass away,*
*And the chiselled shapes to combine in a haze of sun,*
*Till beside a Carrara column there gleamed forth One.*

*She looked not this nor that of those beings divine,*
*But each and the whole – an essence of all the Nine;*
*With tentative foot she neared to my halting-place,*
*A pensive smile on her sweet, small, marvellous face.*

*'Regarded so long, we render thee sad?' said she.*
*'Not you,' sighed I, 'but my own inconstancy!*
*I worship each and each; in the morning one,*
*And then, alas! another at sink of sun.*

*'To-day my soul clasps Form; but where is my troth*
*Of yesternight with Tune: can one cleave to both?'*
*– 'Be not perturbed,' said she. 'Though apart in fame,*
*As I and my sisters are one, those, two, are the same.'*

*– 'But my love goes further – to Story, and Dance, and Hymn,*
*The lover of all in a sun-sweep is fool to whim –*
*Is swayed like a river-weed, as the ripples run!'*
*– 'Nay, wooer, thou sway'st not. These are but phases of one;*

*'And that one is I; and I am projected from thee,*
*One that out of thy brain and heart thou causest to be –*
*Extern to thee nothing. Grieve not, nor thyself becall,*
*Woo where thou wilt; and rejoice thou canst love at all!'*

*Who,*
*And what is he to me? –*
*Amid thick thoughts and memories multitudinous*
*One thought alone brings he.*

*I can recall no word*
*Of anything he did;*
*For me he is a man who died and was interred*
*To leave a pyramid*

*Whose purpose was exprest*
*Not with its first design,*
*Nor till, far Down in Time, beside it found their rest*
*Two countrymen of mine.*

*I know not.*
*He does a finer thing,*

*In beckoning pilgrim feet*
*With marble finger high*
*To where, by shadowy wall and history-haunted street,*
*Those matchless singers lie. . . .*

*– Say, then, he lived and died*
*That stones which bear his name*
*Should mark, through Time, where two immortal Shades abide;*
*It is an ample fame.*

(*above*) Hardy, aged forty-seven

(*below*) Hardy, aged fifty-five

*Far from the Madding Crowd.* It was precisely the right mixture of drama and idyll which had caused people to notice him in the first place. It should have marked the beginning of a period of serene eminence in Hardy's career but it did not. The next ten years were the darkest of his sombre life.

Hardy used to say that he remained 'a child till he was sixteen, a youth till he was five-and-twenty, and a young man till he was nearly fifty'. At the end of 1887 he was in his forty-eighth year and presented a slightly balding version of the small but robust figure which had surprised Emma in the hall at St Juliot nearly twenty years before. The beard, which he had grown soon after he came back from London in 1867, was shaved off in 1890. At the same time, he began to shed more of his dark chestnut hair, and the skin began to contract and then shrivel on his massive skull. By the mid-nineties, Hardy had assumed what Max Beerbohm recalled to Lord David Cecil as 'his old plain face, that had such beauty', which developed but did not basically change for the rest of his life. Although he suffered from some of the hypochondria of the self-obsessed, Hardy's health was generally very good and he took good care of himself. His lean, 5 feet 6½ inch frame was exposed to no excesses: he ate frugally, drank very little and did not smoke at all, and the regular exercise he took on foot and bicycle was exacting but never over-stimulating. The physical transformation in these years reflects an entirely spiritual torment.

Walter Besant and Eliza Lynn

besetting sin of modern ...
are qualified, even contradicted, by an aside, and this particularly in morals and religion.' In the essay, he set out to argue this point in full.

Hardy's view of the writer's first duty was the honest portrayal of life: 'Life being a physiological fact, its honest portrayal must be largely concerned with, for one thing, the relations of the sexes'; the history of some sexual relationships would in time raise questions on accepted morality; and these, in turn, issues concerning religion, the source of the conventions governing morality. Hardy thought that there was a very great deal to be said about life in the last quarter of the nineteenth century and plenty of talent available to say it but that writers were constantly inhibited and sometimes completely frustrated by what Stephen had warned him of over *The Return of the Native,* the need to avoid anything '"dangerous" for a family magazine'. Hardy despised, of course, writing that was gratuitously prurient or scandalous. All he wanted was freedom to carry a human drama to its natural conclusion and not to be compelled either to veil the truth or to turn aside halfway through in order to avoid shocking his readers by what they did not know or upsetting them by what they did not want to hear. Yet this is precisely what he sometimes had to do in the serial versions of his novels. 'If the true artist ever weeps', he wrote towards the end of 'Candour in English Fiction', 'it probably is then, when he first discovers the fearful price that he has to pay for the privilege of writing in the English language.'

(*above*) West Stafford church, where Tess and Angel Clare were married

(*below*) The gateway of Stalbridge House, all that remains of 'Stapleford Park', the scene of 'Squire Petrick's Lady'

(*above right*) The inn at Marnhull on which Hardy based 'Rolliver's'. The notice reads: 'Elizabeth Jarvis, licensed to sell & retail beer, ale and cider to be consumed off the premises'

(*below right*) Marnhull, the 'Marlott' of *Tess of the d'Urbervilles*. 'The Pure Drop' inn is on the right

As Hardy's popularity reached dizzy heights in the 1890s, the bonds of public taste grew tighter. When he sent *A Group of Noble Dames* to the *Graphic* in June 1890, the editor's response was firm. 'Now', wrote Arthur Locker, 'what do you propose to do? Will you write an entirely fresh story, or will you take the "Noble Dames" and alter them to suit our taste?' Hardy set about the necessary bowdlerisation indifferently but with a bad grace, marking the manuscript with waspish remarks, such as 'solely on account of the tyranny of Mrs Grundy' against one of the excisions from 'Squire Petrick's Lady'.

*A Group of Noble Dames* did not mean much to Hardy either artistically or in terms of effort. Two of the stories had been written earlier and the rest were added quickly with no purpose but to entertain. *Tess of the d'Urbervilles* was a different matter, and he fought hard to get it published in its original form.

Tillotson's Fiction Bureau had asked Hardy for a serial in 1888.

THERE,S A FORTUNE FOR YOU IN JOHN. III.16. Go for it. No Lawyers
NOW IS THE ACCEPTED TIME

(*opposite above*) An example of the text-writer's art. In this instance he seems to have been followed by a graffitist of a different kind.

(*opposite below*) The cottage by the church at Evershot, where Tess stopped for breakfast on her walk from 'Flintcomb-Ash' to visit Clare's parents at Beaminster

By the autumn of the following year he had completed about half of it, then entitled 'Too Late Beloved', which Tillotson's sent straight to the printer. It was not until proofs were returned that they realised what they had got. Tillotson's was still ruled by the spirit of its Congregationalist founder W. F. Tillotson, and the editor immediately insisted that certain episodes, notably Tess's seduction and the midnight baptism of her child Sorrow, would have to go. Hardy refused, and the agreement was cancelled.

The editors of two other magazines made similar conditions. Hardy rejected them and worked on to complete the novel exactly as he had conceived it, apparently willing to martyr his career, as his heroine martyred herself, for the sake of truth. But when he had finished the book Hardy saw that his story of the dispossessed rural poor, the cruelty of which men were capable particularly towards the weakest, the brutality of many of the dictates of their religion and the hopelessness of natural purity in a society governed by them would stand in reduced outline even if the offending passages were taken out. So with 'cynical amusement' he recast most of *Tess of the d'Urbervilles* in what he knew would be an acceptable form before sending it to the *Graphic*, which began serialisation in July 1891.

The alterations to the serial version of *Tess* form a strange catalogue of late-Victorian sensibilities. The main result, of course, was that the novel contained no sex: Tess was not seduced but put through a bogus marriage ceremony; she did not bear a child, and this in turn disposed of the delicate question of the baptism; and at the end she went to live with Alec at Sandbourne on explicitly platonic terms. On less central points: Angel Clare was denied the varied pleasure of grappling with the Talbothays dairymaids by

(*right*) The Turberville window in the south aisle of Bere Regis church. *Within the window under which the bedstead stood were the tombs of the family, covering in their dates several centuries. They were canopied, altar-shaped, and plain; their carvings being defaced and broken; their brasses torn from the matrices, the rivet-holes remaining like martin-holes in a sand-cliff. Of all the reminders that she had ever received that her people were socially extinct there was none so forcible as this spoliation.*

immense length of

the pinnacled tower of the College, &, more to the right, the tower & gables of the ancient hospice where to this day the pilgrim may receive his dole of bread & ale. Behind the city swept the rotund upland of St Catherine's Hill, further off, landscape beyond landscape, till the horizon was lost in the radiance of the sun hanging above it.

Against these far stretches of country rose, in front of the other city edifices, a large red brick building, with level grey roofs, & rows of short barred windows bespeaking captivity — the whole contrasting greatly by its regularity with the quaint irregularities of the Gothic erections. It was somewhat disguised from the road in passing it by yews & evergreen oaks, but it was visible enough up here. From the middle of the building a flat-topped octagonal tower ascended against the east horizon, & viewed from this spot, on its shady side & against the light it seemed a blot on the city's beauty. Yet it was with this blot & not with the beauty, that the two gazers were concerned.

Upon the cornice of the tower a tall staff was fixed, & on this their eyes were rivetted on it. A few minutes after the hour had struck something shot up the staff, & extended itself upon the breeze. It was a black flag.

"Justice" was done, & the President of the Immortals (in Aeschylean phrase) had ended his sport with Tess. And the D'Urberville Knights & Dames slept on in their tombs unknowing. The two speechless gazers bent themselves down to the earth, as if in prayer, & remained thus a long time, absolutely motionless: the flag continued to wave silently. As soon as they had strength they arose, joined hands again, & went on.

The End.

(*opposite*) The last page of the manuscript of *Tess of the d'Urbervilles*

being sent to fetch a wheelbarrow in which to convey them through the flood at arms' length; and it is made clear that his invitation to Izz Huett to go and live with him in Brazil was intended as a joke. The text-writer in chapter 12 was another victim of Mrs Grundy, presumably because she could not bear to see the seventh Commandment in print, except on Sundays. She never did, for when the scene was restored to the book version of the novel he paints 'THOU, SHALT, NOT, COMMIT' – and Tess moves on with her eyes demurely on the ground. In the first book-edition of *Tess*, published largely as Hardy originally wrote it, the seduction scene was still giving trouble and had to be accounted for by the additionally unedifying expedient of having Tess drugged by Alec from a two-gallon jar of spirits.

*Tess* caused an immediate sensation and sold as no novel by Hardy had ever sold before. It put him in a public glare of a kind that he had never previously had to endure. It brought him many letters, some sincere ones asking for advice, others pages of closely argued abuse. Most were burnt. While the general tone of the more responsible reviewers was that the novel was his best so far, others ranged from wild superlatives – 'One of the greatest novels of this century ... a monumental work' – to vitriol – 'Mr Hardy has told an extremely

Heredity

*I am the family face;*
*Flesh perishes, I live on,*
*Projecting trait and trace*
*Through time to times anon,*
*And leaping from place to place*
*Over oblivion.*

*The years-heired feature that can*
*In curve and voice and eye*
*Despise the human span*
*Of durance – that is I;*
*The eternal thing in man,*
*That heeds no call to die.*

(*below*) Portraits of Julia (left) and Frances Turberville on the walls of the staircase at Woolbridge Manor. *He looked up, and perceived two life-size portraits on panels built into the masonry. As all visitors to the mansion are aware, these paintings represent women of middle age, of a date some two hundred years ago, whose lineaments once seen can never be forgotten. The long pointed features, narrow eye, and smirk of the one, so suggestive of merciless treachery; the bill-hook nose, large teeth, and bold eye of the other, suggesting arrogance to the point of ferocity, haunt the beholder afterwards in his dreams. . . .*
*The unpleasantness of the matter was that, in addition to their effect upon Tess, her fine features were unquestionably traceable in these exaggerated forms.*

…able manner', Hardy

novel-writing …
to be shot at.' But he did not give up just yet.

For one thing, Tillotson's wanted a serial in place of the one they had lost. Hardy never based more than one novel in the same part of Wessex, and from the wide and varied scene of *Tess of the d'Urbervilles* he now moved to the Isle of Portland. Portland was a highly individual community, where marriage was a contract for seven years voidable thereafter by either party and where marriages were commonly preceded by periods of cohabitation to test the prospects of their fertility. Hardy could doubtless have made a very shocking story of *The Well-Beloved,* and indeed 'certain critics affected to find unmentionable moral atrocities in its pages'. Instead, he provided Tillotson's with something 'short and slight, and written entirely with a view to serial publication' and submitted a detailed synopsis before he committed himself to writing it.

*The Well-Beloved,* nevertheless, is the most interesting of Hardy's less regarded novels. The idea for it had been in his mind since at least 1884 when he had noted that 'The story of a face which goes through three generations or more, would make a fine novel or poem of the passage of Time. The differences in personality to be ignored.' Hardy took a deep interest in genetics, and hereditary tendencies of the most luckless type play a part in both *Tess* and *Jude the Obscure,* but his idea that romantic love is subjective, summarised for the purpose of the novel in lines from Shelley's 'Epipsychidion',

> In many mortal forms I rashly sought
> The shadow of that idol of my thought,

had been present in his work long before – in 'Amabel' and other

The 'Brown House' of *Jude the Obscure.* The Red House Barn stood at the junction of the Berkshire Ridgeway and the road from Newbury to Wantage. From the roof, Jude thought he could see Oxford

Grove's Place, Shaftesbury, where Sue and Phillotson lived. *'It is so antique and dismal'*, says Sue, *'that it depresses me dreadfully. Such houses are very well to visit, but not to live in – I feel crushed into the earth by the weight of so many previous lives there spent.'*

poems of the 1860s in which Hardy dreamed of unattainable and largely unknown women; in Boldwood's silent passion for Bathsheba, although he knows virtually nothing about her; in Eustacia's love for Clym before she has ever set eyes on him – and was carried on to Jude Fawley, who realised precisely what Arabella was before he married her but 'For his own soothing . . . kept up a factitious belief in her. His idea of her was the thing of most consequence, not Arabella herself.'

When Harper's asked Hardy for a serial in 1893, he had to assure them that 'it would be a tale that could not offend the most fastidious maiden'. Even at this stage, however, the novel he had in mind was gloomy enough, based on a note he had made in April 1888: 'A short story of a young man – "who could not go to Oxford" – His struggles and ultimate failure. Suicide. There is something [in this] the world ought to be shown, and I am the one to show it to them.' During 1892 and 1893 he drafted a story exclusively on these lines, then called 'The Simpletons', but by April 1894 he found it necessary to warn Harper's that 'the development of the story was carrying him into unexpected fields and that he was afraid to predict its

They refused
but when the manuscript arrived with the editor
certain changes, with the result – as with *Tess* – that *Jude the Obscure* was entirely sexless. The fruits of Jude's unsanctified alliance with Sue Bridehead were passed off as orphans.

Through his second wife Hardy let it be known that 'Speaking generally, there is more autobiography in a hundred lines of Mr Hardy's poetry than in all the novels.' He qualified this in correspondence with Clive Holland, who was trying to write a biography of him, when he said, 'If you read the ... *Collected Poems* you will gather more personal particulars than I could give you in an interview, circumstances not being so veiled in the verse as in the novels.' Over *Jude the Obscure,* which has exercised inquirers for links between Hardy's life and work more than any other novel, he insisted that 'there is not a scrap of personal detail in it'. On the whole, he should be believed.

Yet some of the bitterness of Jude's frustrated academic and clerical ambitions must be Hardy's own. The first note for the story of *Jude,* quoted above, continues '– though I was not altogether hindered going, at least to Cambridge, and could have gone up easily at five-and-twenty'. According to a nephew of Horace Moule's, Hardy did have a sense of inferiority about not having been to a university. If this implies that he once tried to enter Oxford, he succeeded in covering his tracks completely. But when he visited Oxford in 1864 in connection with Blomfield's work on the chapel of the Radcliffe Infirmary he would have arrived, like Jude, after studying half the night in his lodgings, full of reverence for the temple of the learning he was striving so hard for and, if he saw much of the smug dons and idle undergraduates, would have gone away wondering whether they were really the sort of people for whom the place was intended.

During the same visit to Oxford, Hardy went out to Great

Hardy's sketch of the old church in Great Fawley, which he made on a visit in the autumn of 1864

Fawley to look at the graves of his grandmother's family in the churchyard and to sketch the old church, which was soon to be demolished. Fawley is a singularly austere village, but he made several visits, including at least one with Emma in the 1870s, before his final peregrination of the topography of *Jude* in October 1892.

The other biographical spectre that has been called up to elucidate *Jude the Obscure* is Tryphena Sparks as the inspiration of the character of Sue Bridehead. Hardy himself started this particular hare when he said in the preface that some of the circumstances of the novel had been suggested by the death of a woman in 1890. This has been taken to be a reference to Tryphena, by then Mrs Charles Gale, who, sure enough, died at Topsham in March that year, although what this event can have suggested for the purposes of the novel is far from clear. The similarities between Jude and Sue on the one hand and Hardy and Tryphena on the other appear to be that both couples were cousins and that both the ladies were schoolmistresses. As nothing of substance is known about the character of Tryphena or of Hardy's relationship with her it is impossible to press the likeness further. In any case, Hardy also implied in a letter to Gosse that Sue's character owed something to Florence Henniker, one of his fashionable friends of the 1890s, and in the eyes of anyone but a creative artist just about as unlike Tryphena as it is possible for two women to be. Hardy's mature method was that of all great writers, drawing alike on experience, imagination and wide-ranging perception for his purpose, which was not to provide a personal memorandum.

In spite of the nuptial labyrinth in *Jude the Obscure,* the point of it remains the tragedy of the hero's ambitions, defeated by prejudicial circumstances, not least his own tendencies to drink, melancholia and excessive sensuality. Nevertheless, it was Hardy's unflattering references to Christian matrimony, 'a sordid contract, based on material convenience', which caught the public eye when the novel was published and caused him finally to part company with most of the critics. 'It is simply', said the *New York Bookman,* 'one of the most objectionable books that we have ever read in any language whatsoever.' In England, in a review entitled 'The Anti-Marriage League', Mrs Oliphant observed that 'it unconsciously affords us the strongest illustration of what Art can come to when given over to the exposition of the unclean'. A lecturer in Liverpool, discussing Hardy's work at length, said 'this author has a curious mania for exploiting sewers; filth and defilement he faces with the calm, unshrinking countenance of a Local Board labourer'. The Bishop of Wakefield wrote to the *Yorkshire Post* to say that 'I bought one of Mr Hardy's novels, but was so disgusted with its insolence and indecency that I threw it into the fire', and privately to W. H. Smith in London, with the result that the book was quietly withdrawn from their circulating library.

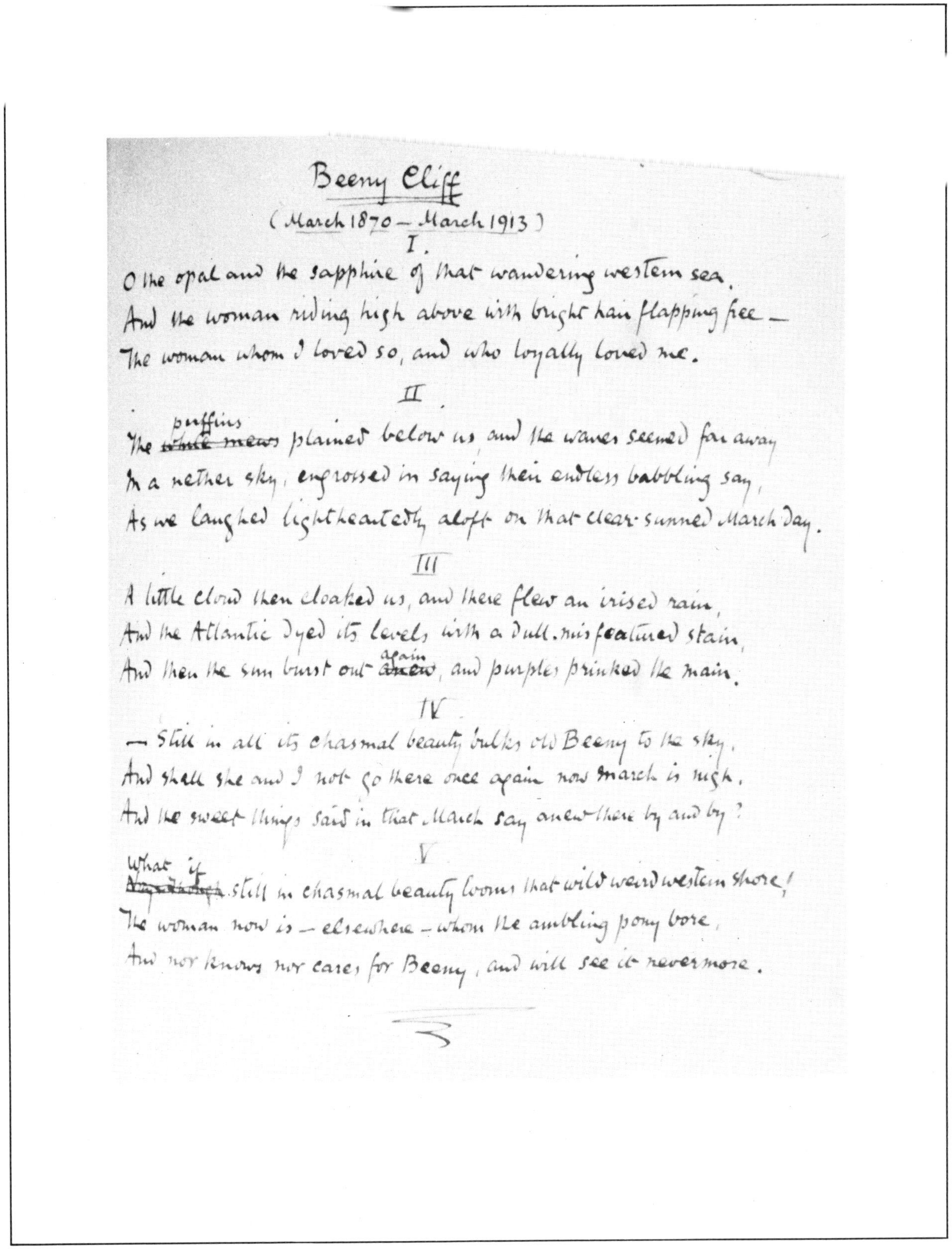

## Beeny Cliff

(March 1870 – March 1913)

I.

O the opal and the sapphire of that wandering western sea,
And the woman riding high above with bright hair flapping free –
The woman whom I loved so, and who loyally loved me.

II.

The ~~white mews~~ puffins plained below us, and the waves seemed far away
In a nether sky, engrossed in saying their endless babbling say,
As we laughed lightheartedly aloft on that clear-sunned March day.

III

A little cloud then cloaked us, and there flew an irised rain,
And the Atlantic dyed its levels with a dull misfeatured stain,
And then the sun burst out ~~anew~~ again, and purples prinked the main.

IV.

– Still in all its chasmal beauty bulks old Beeny to the sky,
And shall she and I not go there once again now March is nigh,
And the sweet things said in that March say anew there by and by?

V

~~[illegible]~~ What if still in chasmal beauty looms that wild weird western shore,
The woman now is – elsewhere – whom the ambling pony bore,
And nor knows nor cares for Beeny, and will see it nevermore.

Wessex Heights.

(1896)

There are some heights in Wessex, shaped as if by a kindly hand
For thinking, dreaming, dying on, and at crises when I stand,
Say, on Ingpen Beacon eastward, or on Wylls-Neck westwardly,
I seem where I was before my birth, and after death may be.

In the lowlands I have no comrade, not even the lone man's friend –
Her who suffereth long and is kind; accepts what he is too weak to mend:
Down there they are dubious and askance; there nobody thinks as I,
But mind-chains do not clank where one's next neighbour is the sky.

In the towns I am tracked by phantoms having weird detective ways –
Shadows of beings who fellowed with the myself of earlier days:
They hang about at places, and they say harsh heavy things –
Men with a frigid sneer, and women with tart disparagings.

Down there I seem to be false to myself, my simple self that was,
And is not now, and I see him watching, wondering what crass cause
Can have merged him into such a strange continuator as this,
Who yet has something in common with himself, my chrysalis.

I cannot go to the great grey Plain; there's a figure against the moon,
Nobody sees it but I, and it makes my breast beat out of tune;
I cannot go to the tall-spired town, being barred by the forms now passed
For everybody but me, in whose long vision they stand there fast.

There's a ghost at Yell'ham Bottom chiding loud at the fall of the night,
There's a ghost in Froom-side Vale – thin lipped and vague, in a shroud of white,
There is one in the railway-train whenever I do not want it near,
I see its profile against the pane, saying what I would not hear.

As for one rare fair woman, I am now but a thought of hers,
I enter her mind and another thought succeeds me that she prefers;
Yet my love for her in its fulness she herself even did not know;
Well, Time cures hearts of tenderness, and now I can let her go.

So I am found on Ingpen Beacon, or on Wylls-Neck to the west,
Or else on homely Bulbarrow, or little Pilsdon Crest,
Where men have never cared to haunt, nor women have walked with me,
And then ghosts keep their distance, and I know some liberty.

(*opposite*) View of Blackmore Vale from Bulbarrow, one of Hardy's 'Wessex Heights'.

d him with

in London, he went out
great glee. 'He said he had just read in some paper that had been sent him with a marked article on literature, or some subject of the sort: "Swinburne planteth, Hardy watereth and Satan giveth the increase".' Swinburne liked and approved of all Hardy's books, especially *Jude*. 'The man who can do such work', he wrote, 'can hardly care about criticism or praise.' Hardy did not, but neither did he expose himself to it again in a novel.

There is no need for excessive piety about Hardy's decision to write no more in prose less than halfway through his career. He was exasperated and exhausted by the problems of serial writing but not broken by them. At one stage in the nineties he considered spending the rest of his days writing harmless society novels. Publicly, he always took his work very lightly. 'The whole thing', Virginia Woolf wrote after a visit to Max Gate in 1926, '– literature, novels etc., all seemed to him an amusement, far away too, scarcely to be taken seriously.' Novels mattered least of all to him. He had started to write them in the first place only because he could find no ear for his poetry. The exhilaration of his first small success with *Under the Greenwood Tree* had led to the major triumph of *Far from the Madding Crowd,* and from there the need to support Emma and himself had taken over. 'For the relief of my necessities, as the Prayer Book puts it', he told Gosse in 1918, 'I began writing novels and made a sort of trade of it.' But the need was now gone. At

A. C. Swinburne

*O that far morning of a summer day*
*When down a terraced street whose pavements lay*
*Glassing the sunshine into my bent eyes,*
*I walked and read with a quick glad surprise*
*New words, in classic guise, –*

*The passionate pages of his earlier years,*
*Fraught with hot sighs, sad laughters, kisses, tears;*
*Fresh-fluted notes, yet from a minstrel who*
*Blew them not naïvely, but as one who knew*
*Full well why thus he blew.*

*I still can hear the brabble and the roar*
*At those thy tunes, O still one, now passed through*
*That fitful fire of tongues then entered new!*
*Their power is spent like spindrift on this shore;*
*Thine swells yet more and more.*

(from 'A Singer Asleep')

(*above*) Emma, aged fifty-six

the age of fifty-six, he could reasonably have expected to die within the next fifteen years, and the small income which he needed seemed more than assured by continuing sales of most of his books, of which the first collected edition was then being prepared.

'What', asked Edmund Gosse in a review of *Jude the Obscure*, 'has Providence done to Mr Hardy that he should rise up in the arable land of Wessex and shake his fist at his Creator?' Leaving aside the generalities behind Hardy's twilight view of life, there was a daily fact under his own roof for thirty-eight years which caused him, if not to despair, then often to lament his existence. This was Emma. 'I feel', he wrote to Sir George Douglas in 1895, 'that a bad marriage is one of the direst things on earth, and one of the cruellest', and he spoke from experience.

No marriage to Thomas Hardy would have been easy. He was a completely private man with a need, evident in the history of his friendships, for occasional personal props but a distaste for real intimacy which excluded even marriage. While his second wife Florence was to play a very special part in his last years with great success, Emma had been faced with an impossible job for which she was unsuited to make any success at all.

Emma was quite unlike Hardy in every way. 'He', T. P. O'Connor recalled, 'was small, frail-looking, sombre; she was full-blown, with an ample figure, a large rubicund face, and a defiantly jolly expression; whether it was good nature or revolt it is impossible to say.' The differences went right through, aggravated in later years by what Hardy called her 'painful delusions' and always by what Emma regarded as his vanity and selfishness.

There was common ground for discontent in their childlessness. Hardy always wanted children and apparently never ceased to hope

(*below*) A garden party at Max Gate *c.* 1900. Hardy is seated in the middle with Emma seated one away from him on his right. Sir Edmund Gosse is seated on the ground at the extreme left-hand side of the photograph

Emma and Hardy on the lawn at Max Gate, *c.*1890

that he might have some. His Will, drawn up in 1922, when he was over eighty and his second wife forty-three, contains full provision for their existence. In the middle 1880s, when it was clear that Emma and he would have no children, they virtually adopted some of her Gifford nephews, and Hardy later took a close interest in his cousin Frank George, who was killed in 1915. If the poem 'At a Bridal' refers specifically to the wedding of one of the women whom Hardy had loved and lost in the 1860s, there was a special irony in the barrenness of his own marriage, for it described the tragedy of that mismating in terms of the children:

> Compounded of us twain as Love designed;
> Rare forms, that corporate now will never be!

There is a similar thought in 'To a Motherless Child', addressed to a daughter of Tryphena Sparks whom Hardy met when he visited her mother's grave at Topsham in July 1890.

Emma began to feel excluded from the most important part of Hardy's life very early in their marriage. As he became very famous and fellow celebrities began to descend on Max Gate she gained a little ground as the mistress of the house and locally she was always more popular than he was. Most visitors liked her, although she had a habit of turning the conversation away from the subjects on which they most wanted to hear Hardy. Emma was neither passive nor dim. Her life and Hardy's would have been a great deal easier if she had been. She took an active interest in numerous causes, among them female suffrage, and was present in at least one suffragette demonstration in London; but she was a woman of strict and conventional principle, completely out of sympathy with Hardy's iconoclastic attitudes. Like many of their readers, she was deeply offended by the attacks on religion and marriage in the later novels, and when *Jude the Obscure* was in the press went to see the Director of the British Museum, apparently in the belief that he could stop its publication.

One of his jibes about marriage in *Jude* – 'Fewer women like marriage than you suppose . . . they enter into it for . . . the social advantages it gains them' – was particularly outrageous in Emma's view, for next to his opinions Hardy's family was an embarrassment to her. She never forgot, nor allowed him to forget, that she was a woman of breeding and background who had done herself a social disservice by marrying him. Although they had stayed with his parents at Bockhampton once or twice during the early years of their marriage, neither Thomas II nor Jemima was ever allowed to set foot in Max Gate, even during Jemima's twelve years of widowhood after 1892. Towards the end of her life, when Jemima had been reduced to a beady eye peering from a heap of bedding in a Bath chair, she would be wheeled out to watch the guests arriving at Max Gate for a garden party or some other function but that was as near as she ever got.

In her own way Emma was an embarrassment to Hardy in return, not least as a result of her excursions into literature. Up to *The Woodlanders* she had contributed something to most of the novels as amanuensis and very occasionally by suggesting ideas, for which she received no public recognition. Except for the play *The Famous Tragedy of the Queen of Cornwall*, published in 1923, none of Hardy's works bears any dedication. She became extremely jealous, and one of her 'painful delusions' seems to have been that the more edifying parts, at least, of Hardy's triumph derived from her inspiration. 'I have it all here', she would say, pointing to her generous bosom, 'but I have not the power of expressing it.' Nevertheless, she tried in both poetry and prose, and in 1911 had two small volumes produced by a Dorchester printer. Some of her poems had previously appeared in the *County Chronicle*, like 'Ten Moons':

In misery swirled
   Is this one-moon whirled,
But there's no sorrow or darkness there
   In that mighty Planet where
There is no night.
   Ten moons ever revolving
All matters its long years resolving
   To sweetness and light.

Then there were Hardy's other women. *Wessex Poems*, published in 1898, contained numerous poems about the women Hardy had loved before he met Emma, including one as sensitive and recently

where. In his fifties and ...
several ninetyish beauties. When they showed any interest in writing, he flattered and abetted them. Agnes Grove, for example, daughter of General Augustus Pitt-Rivers, with whom Hardy danced in the Larmer Gardens, her father's celebrated pleasure grounds at Rushmore, wrote a little. While Emma's apocalyptic visions, *Spaces*, had to be whispered abroad at her own expense by a local printer, Agnes's tract on manners, *The Social Fetich*, was brought out with a warm dedication to Hardy by no less a publisher than Smith, Elder.

Poor Emma did not show up well beside the 'seductive' Agnes, the 'laughing-eyed' Duchess of Manchester or the 'handsome' Lady Jeune. On one of Hardy's increasingly rare appearances in society with Emma, at the Duchess of Sutherland's, a guest remembered him coming in and 'in his wake an excessively plain, dowdy, high-stomached woman, with her hair drawn back in a tight little knot'.

In the nineties, Hardy's spirit reached its lowest. The three 'In Tenebris' poems, each with a motto from the Vulgate – 'My heart is smitten, and withered like grass', 'Why do the heathen rage, and the people imagine a vain thing?', 'Woe is me that I sojourn in Mesech, that I dwell in the tents of Kedar. My soul hath long

*I am stopped from hoping what I have hoped before –*
*Yes, many a time! –*
*To dance with that fair woman yet once more*
*As in the prime*
*Of August, when the wide-faced moon looked through*
*The boughs at the faery lamps of the Larmer Avenue.*

*I could not, though I should wish, have over again*
*That old romance,*
*And sit apart in the shade as we sat then*
*After the dance*
*The while I held her hand, and, to the booms*
*Of contrabassos, feet still pulsed from the distant rooms.*

*I could not. And you do not ask me why.*
*Hence you infer*
*That what may chance to the fairest under the sky*
*Has chanced to her.*
*Yes. She lies white, straight, features marble-keen,*
*Unapproachable, mute, in a nook I have never seen.*

*There she may rest like some vague goddess, shaped*
*As out of snow;*
*Say Aphrodite sleeping; or bedraped*
*Like Kalupso;*
*Or Amphitrite stretched on the Mid-sea swell,*
*Or one of the nine grown stiff from thought. I cannot tell!*

Agnes Grove.
Hardy met her at Rushmore in September 1895. She was the last woman with whom he ever danced, with such abandon that their fellow promenaders 'eyed them with a mild surmise as to whether they had been drinking or not'. 'Concerning Agnes' was written after her death in December 1926

(*above*) Florence Henniker

(*below*) Hardy's drawing for 'Amabel' in *Wessex Poems*. It suggests life running out towards death, while the soul, represented by the butterflies, is outside time.

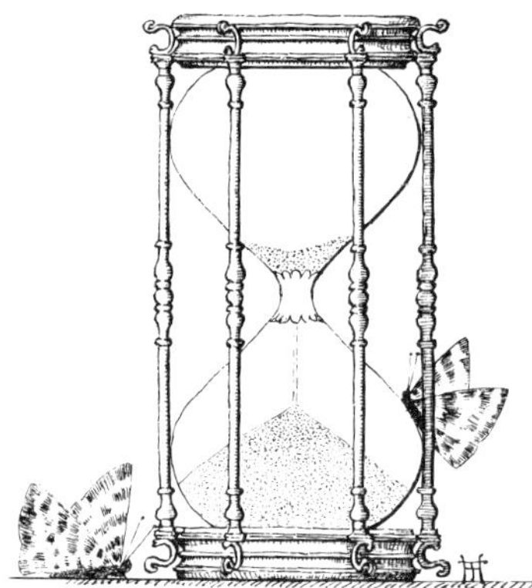

dwelt with him that hateth peace' – show him stunned by a series of blows, utterly out of sympathy with the political jingoism of the time, then approaching its climax with Queen Victoria's jubilee, and regretting that he had lived to look back on the happiness of his childhood. In the depths, he was lucky in one of his new friends, Florence Henniker, whom he met in 1893 and immediately found a 'charming, *intuitive* woman'.

Florence's bookish father, Lord Houghton, had often invited Hardy to stay at his house in Yorkshire. He had accepted as early as the autumn of 1880, but his haemorrhage prevented him going. When he eventually met Florence in Dublin, where she was helping her wifeless brother the viceroy, she was thirty-eight and had published the first of her mildly talented novels. Within two weeks of their meeting a vigorous correspondence had begun, which lasted until Florence's death in 1923. 'I much desire to go somewhere with you,' Hardy wrote on 3 June 1893, and he duly did, to theatres and galleries in London and meetings in the country, halfway between Max Gate and Florence's house at Southsea.

As with Agnes Grove, Hardy hung his hat on Florence's literary ambitions and wrote an adulatory article about her in the *Illustrated London News* in August 1894. 'Her note of individuality,' he said, 'without which neither aristocrat nor democrat, fair woman nor foul, has any right to take a stand before the public as author, may be called that of emotional imaginativeness, lightened by a quick sense of the odd, and by touches of observation lying midway between wit and humour.'

Hardy pressed on and helped Florence with a short story, 'The Spectre of the Real'. Much of it was Hardy's own work and harks back to 'The Poor Man and the Lady'. So did the friendship, for Hardy, no longer poor, was still timid, and Florence, although a grass widow circulating on the fringe of the morally uninhibited Marlborough House Set, was blamelessly married. By 1896, when Hardy placed her among the phantoms of 'Wessex Heights', he had given up hope of anything more than her occasional companionship:

> As for one rare fair woman, I am now but a thought of hers,
> I enter her mind and another thought succeeds me that she prefers;
> Yet my love for her in its fullness she herself even did not know;
> Well, time cures hearts of tenderness, and now I can let her go.

People found it hard to accept Hardy as a poet. He did not expect much himself and offered to pay the cost of producing *Wessex Poems*. 'The illustrations', he told Edward Clodd, 'had for me in preparing them a sort of illegitimate interest – that which arose from their being a novel amusement, and a wholly gratuitous performance which could not profit me anything, and probably would do me harm.' The drawings are beautiful pieces of draughtsmanship

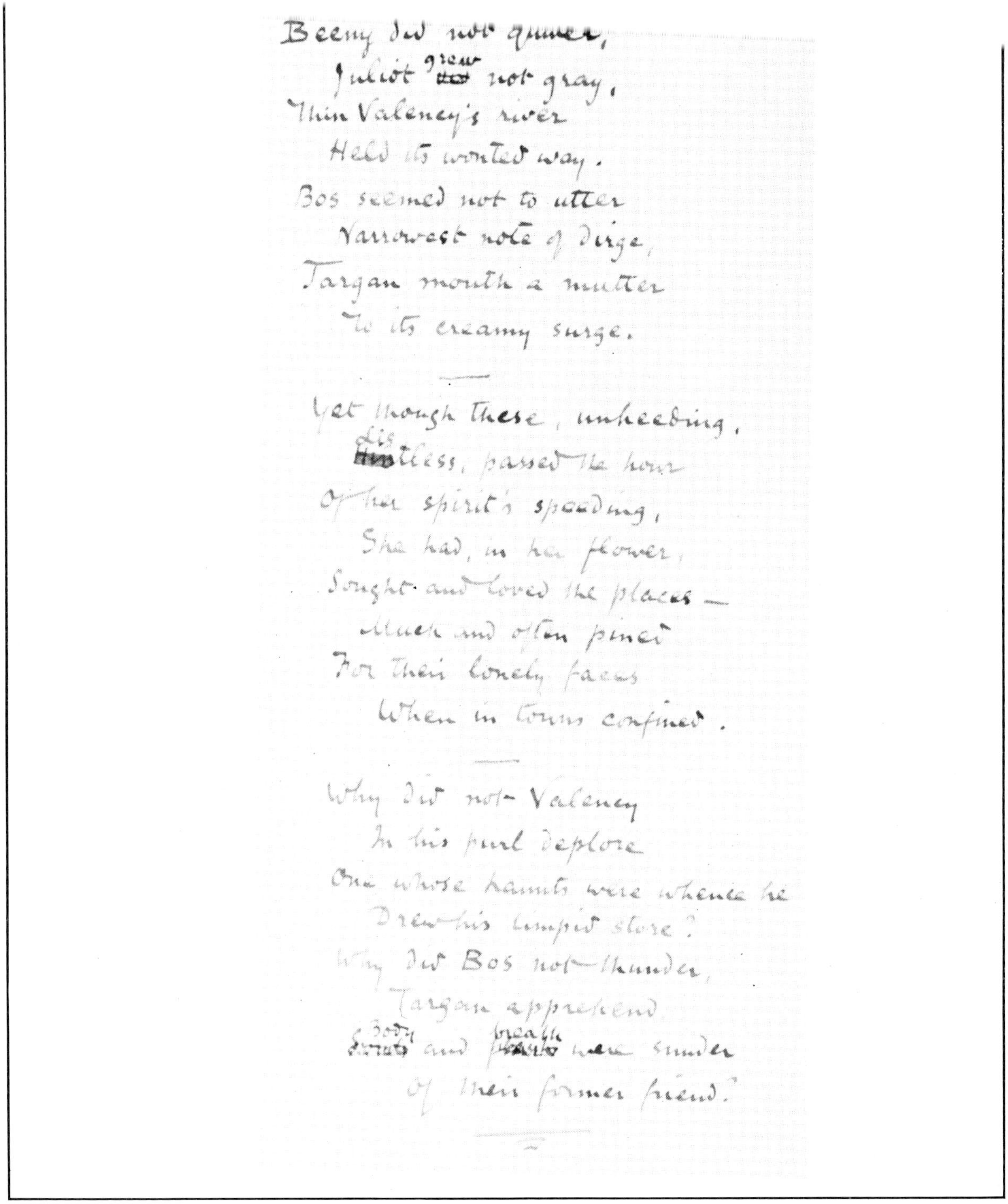

Beeny did not quiver,
Juliot grew not gray,
Thin Valency's river
Held its wonted way.
Bos seemed not to utter
Narrowest note of dirge,
Targan mouth a mutter
To its creamy surge.

—

Yet though these, unheeding,
Listless, passed the hour
Of her spirit's speeding,
She had, in her flower,
Sought and loved the places—
Much and often pined
For their lonely faces
When in towns confined.

—

Why did not Valency
In his purl deplore
One whose haunts were whence he
Drew his limpid store?
Why did Bos not thunder,
Targan apprehend
Body and breath were sunder
Of their former friend?

—



*(opposite)* The Vallency Valley.

## A New Year's Eve in War Time.

I.
Phantasmal fears,
And the flap of the flame,
And the throb of the clock,
And a loosened slate,
And the blind night's drone,
Which tiredly the spectral pines intone.

II
And the blood in my ears
Strumming always the same,
And the gable-cock
With its fitful grate,
And myself, alone.

III
The twelfth hour nears
Hand-hid, as in shame;
I undo the lock,
And listen, & wait
For the Young Unknown.

IV.
In the dark there careers –
As if Death astride came
To numb all with his knock –
A horse at mad rate
Over rut & stone.

V.
No figure appears,
No call of my name,
No sound but "Tic-toc"
Without check. Past the gate
It clatters – is gone.

VI.
What rider it bears
There is none to proclaim;
And the Old Year has struck,
And, scarce animate,
The New makes moan.

VII.
Maybe that "More Tears! –
More Famine & Flame –
More Severance & Shock!"
Is the order from Fate
That the ~~[illegible]~~ Rider bears on
~~[illegible]~~ To pale Europe; & tiredly the pines intone.

1916.

William Blake's 'Pity'.
Hardy wrote to Sir Sydney Cockerell from Max Gate about the poem 'A New Year's Eve in War-time':
*'The incident of the horse galloping past precisely at the stroke of midnight between the old and new year is, by the way, true; it happened here, and we never learnt what horse it was. It is strange that you should have lighted upon the Blake picture which in some respects almost matches the verses.'*

(*opposite*) Augustus John's portrait of Hardy, 1923. John wrote of the sittings at Max Gate: An atmosphere of great sympathy and almost complete understanding at once established itself between us, though the veneration in which I held Hardy impeded to some extent the natural expression of my response to his quite lovable personality. This on his side was counterbalanced by a gracious and delicate consideration which, while it put me at my ease, left me fairly inarticulate. I wonder which of us was the more naïve!
When Hardy saw the portrait he said: 'I don't know whether that is how I look or not, but that is how I *feel*.'

and range from simple illustrations of the subjects of individual poems to rather ponderous symbolism, like the one for 'Amabel', and the completely inscrutable, like the view of Combe Eweleaze with a pair of spectacles laid upon it for 'In a Eweleaze near Weatherbury'.

Most of the critics were predisposed to look at anything Hardy wrote with interest if not respect, but some of them were appalled by *Wessex Poems*. 'As we read this curious and wearisome volume', said the *Saturday Review*, 'these many slovenly, slipshod, uncouth verses, stilted in sentiment, poorly conceived and worse wrought, our respect lessens to vanishing point.' Critical estimates of his poetry were never unanimous, although before long any poem which Hardy submitted to a newspaper or magazine was accepted with rapture. Hardy was always surprised and pleased by this but his pleasure was measured by the suspicion that it was his name as much as the quality of the poetry that was valued. He was disappointed too that even at the end of his life, when his novels belonged to the new literature of an earlier generation, he was still mentioned in general reviews as 'Thomas Hardy, the novelist', rarely 'the poet'.

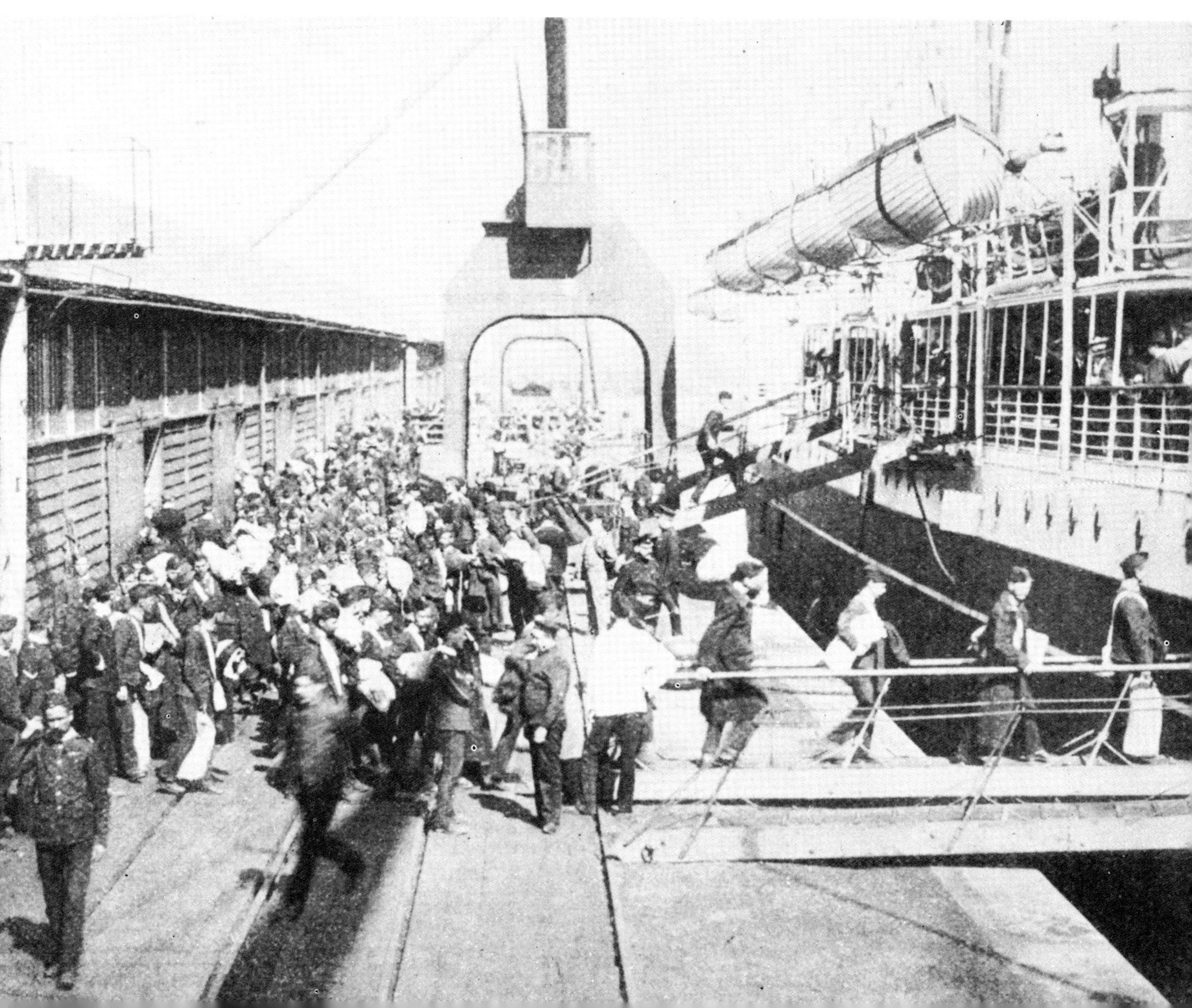

Troops embarking on the S.S. *Gaul* for South Africa at Southampton in the autumn of 1899.

and no

the means

liberty', he wrote, 'we fight for the Transvaal Funds, and gold! Why should not Africa be free, as is America?' During a bicycling tour in October 1899 he saw troops embarking for the Cape at Southampton. He identified Southampton with many previous hostilities, from the landing of Vespasian to the departure of Henry V for Harfleur and the Agincourt campaign, and asked:

> 'How long, O striving Teutons, Slavs, and Gaels
> Must your wroth reasonings trade on lives like these,
>
> That are as puppets in a playing hand? –
> When shall the saner softer polities
> Whereof we dream, have sway in each proud land
> And patriotism, grown Godlike, scorn to stand
> Bondslave to realms, but circle earth and seas?'

'Departure' contains the essence of Hardy's thinking about war and the – to him – obvious alternative in internationalism. Even after the 1914-18 war, he remained optimistic that he would live to see patriotism not confined to realms but circling the earth. Meanwhile, he spent most of the next ten years on a work which set out to show the 'rulers of Europe in their desperate struggle to maintain their dynasties rather than to benefit their peoples' in his epic drama *The Dynasts*.

The gestation of *The Dynasts* was far longer than that of any other of his works. Hardy's first note for 'A Ballad of the Hundred Days. Then another of Moscow. Others of earlier campaigns – forming altogether an Iliad of Europe from 1789 to 1815, dates from 1875, and the idea was never far from his mind until he laid down his pen on the third volume of *The Dynasts* in September 1907.

When T. E. Lawrence got to know Hardy in 1923, he was struck by the extent to which he was absorbed in the Napoleonic era: 'Napoleon is a real man to him,' Lawrence told Robert Graves, '. . . he lives in his period, and thinks of it as *the* great war.' Hardy certainly got as close to it as he could: as a young man in London he had heard Palmerston, who was War Secretary in the years leading up to Waterloo, speak in the House of Commons; on many visits to the Royal Hospital at Chelsea, he had talked to men who had campaigned with Wellington; he had inspected the field of Waterloo and tried to find the exact site of the Duchess of Richmond's ball on the eve of the battle; at the funeral of Louis Napoleon in July 1879, he had noted the profile of Prince Napoleon – 'Complexion dark, sallow, even sinister: a round project-

(*above*) Veterans of Waterloo in the Royal Hospital, Chelsea, June 1880.
The Pensioner seated on the left is Naish Hanney, whom Hardy met on 27 October 1878: 'He enlisted in 1807 or 1808, served under Sir John Moore in the Peninsula, through the Retreat, and was at Waterloo. It was extraordinary to talk and shake hands with a man who had shared in that terrible winter march to Coruña, and had seen Moore face to face.'

ing chin: countenance altogether extraordinarily remindful of Boney'; he had carried the growing idea with him to Italy in 1887, and on the roof of Milan Cathedral conceived the scene of Napoleon's coronation; and throughout he had continued to read widely in the history of the epoch, rehearsed a section of it in *The Trumpet-Major,* and all the while slowly developed the philosophical scheme under which he was to interpret it.

Hardy needed a canvas large enough for a full-size demonstration of the Immanent Will in action. His concept of the power behind existence was first expressed in 'Hap', written in 1866:

> – Crass Casualty obstructs the sun and rain,
> And dicing Time for gladness casts a moan....
> These purblind Doomsters had as readily strown
> Blisses about my pilgrimage as pain.

It later appeared in other forms, like Eustacia Vye's 'colossal Prince of the World, who had framed her situation and shaped her lot', or the 'President of the Immortals', who had made Tess his plaything. In 1881, he had decided that Napoleon should be presented as its chattel also: 'Mode for historical drama. Action mostly automatic; reflex movement etc. Not the result of what is called *motive,* though always ostensibly so, even to the actors' own consciousness'.

complaint was a

> But O, the intolerable antilogy
> Of making figments feel!

Yet there is present in the 'After Scene' of *The Dynasts* the notion that the world can be made better by human effort and that the collective volition of men might even inform the Immanent Will. Hardy returned to earth to make this point in a poem 'A Plaint to Man', written three years after *The Dynasts* was finished:

> The fact of life with dependence placed
> On the human heart's resource alone,
> In brotherhood bonded close and graced
>
> With loving-kindness fully blown,
> And visioned help unsought, unknown.

Hardy did not see much help towards this end in what he called in *The Dynasts* 'a local cult called Christianity'. In a companion poem to 'A Plaint to Man', 'God's Funeral', he considered the development of Christian theology from the bellicose teaching of the Old Testament to the apologetic gropings of modern scholars. In 1897 he had written to Edward Clodd:

> The older one gets the more deplorable seems the effect of that terrible, dogmatic ecclesiasticism – Christianity so called (but really Paulinism *plus* idolatry) – on morals and true religion: a dogma with which the real teaching of Christ has hardly anything in common.... If the doctrines of the supernatural were quietly abandoned tomorrow by the Church, and 'reverence and love for an ethical ideal' alone retained, not one in ten thousand would object to the readjustment, while the enormous bulk of thinkers excluded by the old teaching would be brought into the fold, and our venerable old churches and cathedrals would become the centres of emotional life that they once were.

With this respect for what he chose to regard as the essence of Christianity went Hardy's weakness for some of the accidentals of the Church of England. Beside its architecture and music, he remained fond enough at the age of sixty-five of the matchless language of the King James Version to bicycle seventeen miles over rough and hilly roads to read the lesson for his friend Thomas Perkins, Rector of Turnworth.

Edward Clodd, the agnostic and prolific rationalist writer, was

(*opposite*) The roof of Milan Cathedral from the south transept. It was here, in March 1887, that Hardy conceived the scene of Napoleon's coronation for *The Dynasts*.
The picture, in Hardy's photograph album, was bought during the visit.

(*left*) The Rev. Thomas Perkins,

one of the people Hardy got to know around the turn of the century who remained friends until his death. Hardy's peers from the previous generation, like Swinburne, Stephen and Meredith, began to die off when he was in his sixties but they were replaced by younger ones, who eventually included E. M. Forster, Siegfried Sassoon and Walter de la Mare. A. E. Housman was nearer to Hardy in age and temperament and, like him, a late starter. The flavour of *A Shropshire Lad* was much to Hardy's liking, and after it appeared in 1896 he met Housman often in Dorset and Cambridge. Hardy was Housman's outstanding favourite among living writers, although his esteem was limited to a few of the novels and fewer poems. Among Housman's poems Hardy thought most of

(*right*) Winterborne Houghton. Hardy would have bicycled through the village on his way to Turnworth.

(*above left*) A. E. Housman

(*above right*) Sydney Cockerell

'Is My Team Ploughing?' but not so much as to deny himself some amusement in imitating his style:

'Mistress, I dug upon your grave
    To bury a bone, in case
I should be hungry near this spot
When passing on my daily trot.
I am sorry, but I quite forgot
    It was your resting-place.'

Other friendships began in these years on a purely practical basis. Sydney Cockerell, then Director of the Fitzwilliam Museum at Cambridge, appeared on the scene in the first place to advise on some of the problems, like answering in an equitable manner the clamour of museums and libraries for his manuscripts, that beset Hardy as an ageing writer but remained to become one of the confidants of his last years. Florence Emily Dugdale, whom Mrs Henniker had introduced to Hardy, became indispensable first by checking references for *The Dynasts* in the British Museum, then by doing secretarial work for him and Emma, and finally by helping to run Max Gate.

Things did not improve between Hardy and Emma as they reached and passed the age of seventy. They were much alone. At Max Gate they often lived apart, and Hardy continued to go to London for part of each summer. His letters to Emma, full of the practicalities of life, the weather, times of arrival and departure, the health of the cats and sometimes her own, show no sign of real interest. When Emma threatened to join him in London, he was quietly discouraging. When a pretext arose for prolonging his absence, it was often taken.

Emma suffered from the usual complaints of a woman of her age: fatigue, shingles, unaccountable pains, rheumatism and indigestion. On 25 November 1912 she took to her bed to nurse an outbreak of one of them. On the morning of the twenty-seventh Hardy was summoned to her room. He was used to this sort of thing and climbed the back stairs wearily, no doubt framing some restorative invective in his mind, but within five minutes she was dead.

Hardy's wreath was inscribed 'From her lonely husband – with the old affection'. Shortly after Emma's death he found her artless recollections of her early life, their meeting and courtship, reminding him of how happy he had once made her. As he set out on the winter journey which produced his finest poetry, he wanted to feel the same, but he was almost beaten by remorse. He could not put aside the unalterable facts of much of their marriage or forget his own contribution to them. When he came to collect the twenty-one

Florence Emily Dugdale

A Dream or No

*And a maiden abiding*
*Thereat as in hiding;*
*Fair-eyed and white-shouldered, broad-browed and brown-tressed.*

*And of how, coastward bound on a night long ago,*
*There lonely I found her,*
*The sea-birds around her,*
*And other than nigh things uncaring to know.*

*Can she ever have been there,*
*And shed her life's sheen here,*
*The woman I thought a long housemate with me?*

*Does there even a place like Saint-Juliot exist?*
*Or a Vallency Valley,*
*With stream and leafed alley,*
*Or Beeny, or Bos with its flounce flinging mist?*

## At Castle Boterel

*As I drive to the junction of lane and highway,*
*And the drizzle bedrenches the waggonette,*
*I look behind at the fading byway,*
*And see on its slope, now glistening wet,*
*Distinctly yet*

*Myself and a girlish form benighted*
*In dry March weather. We climb the road*
*Beside a chaise. We had just alighted*
*To ease the sturdy pony's load*
*When he sighed and slowed.*

*What we did as we climbed, and what we talked of*
*Matters not much, nor to what it led, –*
*Something that life will not be balked of*
*Without rude reason till hope is dead,*
*And feeling fled.*

*It filled but a minute. But was there ever*
*A time of such quality, since or before,*
*In that hill's story? To one mind never,*
*Though it has been climbed, foot-swift, foot-sore,*
*By thousands more.*

*Primaeval rocks form the road's steep border,*
*And much have they faced there, first and last,*
*Of the transitory in Earth's long order;*
*But what they record in colour and cast*
*Is – that we two passed.*

*And to me, though Time's unflinching rigour,*
*In mindless rote, has ruled from sight*
*The substance now, one phantom figure*
*Remains on the slope, as when that night*
*Saw us alight.*

*I look and see it there, shrinking, shrinking,*
*I look back at it amid the rain*
*For the very last time; for my sand is sinking,*
*And I shall traverse old love's domain*
*Never again.*

. . . O you could not know
That such swift fleeing
No soul foreseeing –
Not even I – would undo me so!

– and, following such separate lives, at his loneliness:

I walked up there to-day
Just in the former way;
Surveyed around
The familiar ground
By myself again:
What difference, then?
Only that underlying sense
Of the look of a room on returning thence.

Yet she haunted him with a reproachful voice:

When I could answer he did not say them;
When I could let him know
How I would like to join in his journeys
Seldom he wished to go.
Now that he goes and wants me with him
More than he used to do,
Never he sees my faithful phantom
Though he speaks thereto.

By the end of 1912 Hardy had realised that, to recall Emma with the warmth he desperately wanted, he would have to revisit the scenes where they had been happiest. 'My Spirit will not Haunt the Mound' pointed the way to St Juliot:

My spirit will not haunt the mound
Above my breast,
But travel, memory-possessed,
To where my tremulous being found
Life largest, best.

On 6 March 1913, forty-three years almost to the day after his first visit, Hardy set out for Cornwall to realise his dream. There he retraced the steps he had trodden beside Emma's pony on their walks and excursions to Beeny Cliff, down the Vallency valley to Boscastle and inland to Launceston. He found the area neither wistful nor changed and returned to Dorset with the ghost of Emma unexorcised:

staff, and the only visitor he could be relied upon not to bite was T. E. Lawrence.
When Wessex died in 1926, Florence wrote to Cockerell: 'Of course he was merely a dog, and not a good dog always, but *thousands* (actually thousands) of afternoons and evenings I would have been alone but for him, and had always him to speak to.'

(*below*) 'Mr Thomas Hardy composing a lyric' by Max Beerbohm, 1913.
When Vere Collins asked Hardy whether he had ever met Beerbohm, he replied: 'No, but I have sat opposite him at a dinner. He has not at all a humorous face, I thought, but rather a melancholy expression.'

In his rapt thought
On that shagged and shaly
Atlantic spot,
And as when first eyed
Draws rein and sings to the swing of the tide.

'What a revenge,' wrote Florence Dugdale, who married Hardy a year later. When the 'Poems of 1912–13' were published in *Satires of Circumstance*, she told Sydney Cockerell that 'I expect the idea of the general reader will be that TH's second marriage is a most disastrous one and that his sole wish is to find refuge in the grave with her with whom alone he found happiness. Well – all things end somewhere.' At the time of their marriage in February 1914 Florence was thirty-five and Hardy seventy-three. There were no illusions about romance: 'it seemed the wisest thing to do,' Hardy said, 'seeing what a right-hand Florence has become to me, and there is a sort of continuity in it, and not a break, she having known my first wife so very well'. Looking back after ten years of marriage, Florence confided to Cockerell that on the day of Emma's death 'I seemed suddenly to leap from youth into dreary middle-age. I suppose because I had no responsibility before.'

One of the ways in which Florence had made herself useful at Max Gate before Emma's death was by protecting Hardy from some of the problems of being the most celebrated of the elders of English literature. The usual trappings of extreme eminence, like the Order of Merit, began to arrive before the war and were followed by a flow of honorary fellowships and degrees, although, unlike such contemporaries as Galsworthy and Kipling, Hardy was never given the Nobel Prize. Florence became extremely good at controlling the flood of uninvited guests which came with them. Those that were invited were always kindly, if very formally, received and, although impressed by Hardy's ripeness and dignity, often surprised at what they found. 'We went on Friday to see Thomas Hardy,' Frances Cornford told Rupert Brooke. 'He was the most touching old dear I have ever seen. We started in terror, but as soon as he entered the room we discovered that he was much more frightened of us than we of him. I never saw anyone so modest, or so needing appreciation.'

When Alfred Austin died in 1913, Hardy was considered along with Rudyard Kipling and Robert Bridges to succeed him as Poet Laureate. Some, like Wilfrid Scawen Blunt, had thought that *The Dynasts* was a bid for the Laureateship. Hardy would almost certainly have refused it because he hated writing to order, although his ability to make a poem of a commemorative verse might have restored the office to something of its prestige under Tennyson. 'The Convergence of the Twain', written for the *Titanic* disaster fund in April 1912, was no jeremiad. 'God himself could not sink this ship,' it had been said and Hardy saw the disaster as the Immanent Will's rebuke to this and what he called in the poem 'the Pride of Life'.

Soon Hardy was asked to write for a public purpose. In September 1914 he was among a group of writers which included Sir Henry Newbolt, John Masefield, H. G. Wells, Arnold Bennett and John Galsworthy, as well as Bridges the new Poet Laureate, called to a meeting by the Government to organise public statements of the British case and principles in the war. Hardy found himself compromised by the views he had already stated in his Boer War poems and developed in *The Dynasts* but he managed to pervade most of his seventeen 'Poems of War and Patriotism' with a conviction of England's duty to stand firm against wanton aggression, while reiterating his compassion for the people driven to battle to satisfy the war-lords' lust for power. One of the first was 'England to Germany in 1914':

'O England, may God punish thee!'
– Is it that Teuton genius flowers
Only to breathe malignity
Upon its friend of earlier hours?
– We have eaten your bread, you have eaten ours,
We have loved your burgs, your pines' green moan,
Fair Rhine-stream, and its storied towers;
Your shining souls of deathless dowers
Have won us as they were our own:

We have nursed no dreams to shed your blood,
We have matched your might not rancorously
Save a flushed few whose blatant mood
You heard and marked as well as we
To tongue not in their country's key;
But yet you cry with face aflame,
'O England, may God punish thee!'
And foul in onward history,
And present sight, your ancient name.

The racial kinship of the English and the Germans was not the only irony which Hardy saw in the war. 'Among the ironies of the time', he wrote to Cockerell in August 1914, 'is the fact that all the nations are praying to the same God. There was a gleam of reason in the old nations when they prayed for deliverance each

day of the battle of Gravelotte in the Franco-Prussian War, when he had been reading Tennyson with Emma in the garden at St Juliot and watched an old man ploughing in the valley below. He had been consoled then by the fact that such simple labour would outlast the devastations of war and disinterred the idea in 1915 for 'In Time of "The Breaking of Nations"':

I

Only a man harrowing clods
  In a slow silent walk
With an old horse that stumbles and nods
  Half asleep as they stalk.

II

Only thin smoke without flame
  From the heaps of couch-grass;
Yet this will go onward the same
  Though Dynasties pass.

III

Yonder a maid and her wight
  Come whispering by;
War's annals will cloud into night
  Ere their story die.

Hardy tried to carry the compassion of his war poems into practice. He adopted a hearty and wholly uncharacteristic guise on visits to German prisoners of war at Dorchester, to whom he sent books in the hope that his example might improve the conditions of British prisoners in Germany. On one occasion he visited their hospital, where 'one Prussian, in much pain, died whilst I was with him – to my great relief, and his own. Men lie helpless here from wounds: in the hospital a hundred yards off other men, English, lie helpless from the same wounds – each scene of suffering caused by the other.'

Hardy had one personal loss to mourn in the war, when his cousin Frank George, a lieutenant in the 5th Dorset Regiment, was killed at Gallipoli on 22 August 1915. George had been Hardy's closest relation in the next generation and he had planned to make him his heir. 'He was', Florence said, '"*our one*", and we had decided to look upon him as a sort of son – although he was exactly my own age, – and to leave him Max Gate, and all sorts of family possessions belonging to T.'

In material terms the war affected Hardy comparatively little. He

(*below*) Frank George, Hardy's second cousin and proposed heir. He was killed in action at Gallipoli on 22 August 1915. The poem 'Before Marching and After' is about him.

The Hardys during a visit to
Edward Clodd at Aldeburgh, 1915

miles per hour – than by bicycle, and occasionally to go and stay with friends in other parts of the country. But the war slowly destroyed his hopes for the ennoblement of man. Afterwards he said that he would never have ended *The Dynasts* in the way he did if he had foreseen the war. The tone of some of his poetry after 1915 became apocalyptic. The imagery of 'A New Year's Eve in War-time' comes straight from the Book of Revelation.

Hardy's involvement with prose did not end altogether in 1895. He went to great lengths revising his work for Macmillan's Wessex Edition in 1912 and at one stage considered rewriting some of his early novels. To judge from the number of manuscript corrections, the general preface to the Wessex Edition meant much to him. Hardy intended it to be a concise *apologia* for his work. It was not enough, however, to protect him from biographers. F.A. Hedgcock's *Thomas Hardy: penseur et artiste,* published in Paris in 1911, particularly offended him, and he consistently refused to sanction an English translation. 'I have no objection to legitimate literary criticism', he told Vere Collins, himself a visitor at Max Gate more pertinacious than welcome, 'but Mr Hedgcock is continually drawing on the novels for description of my character. His dissection would not be in good taste while I am still alive, even if it were true. But it is based chiefly on characters and incidents that are pure invention.' Hedgcock had been left with little choice. He had been granted two interviews at Max Gate while he was writing the book, at which Hardy had refused to say anything about his life while speaking freely of this work. Later would-be biographers, like Clive Holland, were treated with more circumspection. Hardy recoiled at the thought of a full biography and at some stage towards the end of the war decided to take evasive action, in the hope of carrying his privacy beyond the grave.

One of Hardy's notes says: 'Put in Will that I have written no autobiography but that my wife has notes sufficient for a memoir.' She certainly had, for within three weeks of his death there had arrived with Macmillan a typescript of 100,000 words entitled *The Early Life of Thomas Hardy, 1840–1891*, compiled, according to the title-page, 'largely from contemporary notes, letters, diaries, and biographical memoranda, as well as from oral information in conversations extending over many years by Florence Emily Hardy'. Two years later *The Later Years of Thomas Hardy, 1892–1928* arrived from the same hand.

Apart from the closing chapters of the second volume, this work

Imaginary View of Tintagel Castle.
at the Time of the Tragedy.
T. H.
May 1923.


One of Hardy's drawings for *The Famous Tragedy of the Queen of Cornwall*

was largely Hardy's own. As soon as each part of Florence's typescript was complete, he destroyed his manuscript, and later alterations were made in a specially disguised script. Most of the material which Hardy did not incorporate he there and then destroyed. 'I have not been doing much', he wrote to Sir George Douglas in May 1919, '–mainly destroying papers of the last thirty or forty years, and they raise ghosts.'

In the light of the circumstances of its composition, the *Life* is full of private jokes, such as 'so far as is remembered by the present writer' or declarations like 'his absolute refusal at all times to write his reminiscences'. If it is accepted as the work of Florence, the *Life* comes close to Gosse's definition of good biography, 'to delineate a likeness of the earthly pilgrimage of a man'; but, as it is, the likeness is precisely what Hardy wished the world to see and no more, and has drawn a veil over his life which no subsequent biographer has been able to rend.

The *Early Life* and the *Later Years* must thus be regarded as the biggest single task of Hardy's last ten years. It was an appropriate one for the time. 'He seems to have grown so very much older during the last few months,' Florence told Cockerell in 1919, 'which is saddening at times. He forgets things that have happened only a day or two before, and people he has seen or heard from, though of course his memory of his early life is miraculous.' Hardy drew as heavily on his memories for poems as for the *Life*, and poetry was, of course, infinitely more important to him. But of the four hundred or so poems in his last three volumes of collected verse, *Late Lyrics and Earlier*, *Human Shows* and *Winter Words*, only about a quarter can be firmly dated from the twenties. The principal job was selection, revision and arrangement.

One of the few people whose presence invariably livened Hardy up in his eighties was Gertrude Bugler, the leading lady of the much loved Hardy Players. They had been formed in 1908 out of the Dorchester Debating Society, people who, in the words of one of them, 'have long been familiarised with the speech, the dwellings and habits of the characters portrayed in the novels'. Hardy used to say that Mrs Bugler was precisely the physical type he had in mind when he created Eustacia Vye for *The Return of the Native*. She so shone in this and other parts in dramatisations of the novels that she was tempted to leave her butcher's shop in Bridport for the professional stage. Hardy deplored and discouraged the possibility for, he remarked darkly to Augustus John, 'we know what actresses are'.

Hardy was never happy about the professional productions of his novels. Quite apart from the fact that they led to undignified squabbles over copyright and disagreements over the way the adaptations were done, the dramatised novel was simply a form which he quite disbelieved in. He had prepared outlines for one or two plays of his own but always abandoned them when he saw that play-writing would present him with all the problems of serials, structural and substantial, writ large.

*The Famous Tragedy of the Queen of Cornwall*, a last act of homage and expiation to Emma, was written specifically for the Hardy Players and not originally intended for publication in any other form. The idea of writing something based on the legend of Tristram and Iseult had come to him first during the dreamy summer of 1870 after his first visit to St Juliot. It was revived, with encouragement from Sydney Cockerell, after a visit to Cornwall with Florence in September 1916, although not completed until 1923. 'I visited the place', he wrote afterwards, 'forty-four years ago, with an Iseult of my own, and of course she was mixed in the vision of the other.'

Hardy would have liked to see his other celebration of Cornwall set to music. 'I have thought *A Pair of Blue Eyes* would be good for music', he wrote to Sir Edward Elgar in 1913, 'as it would furnish all the voices and has a distinct and central heroine, with a wild background of cliffs and sea.' But the war delayed any collaboration between them, and the idea was not revived afterwards. Although many of his poems have been set to music by various composers, it is a pity that there are not more and indeed that some, like Gustav

The Prince of Wales, later King Edward VIII, after lunch at Max Gate on 20 July 1923. 'The main characteristic of the visit', Hardy said, 'was its easy informality.'

1912–13' is as powerful as that of Wilhelm Müller's *Winterreise* to which Schubert's music has given an awesome fascination beyond the meaning of the words.

During the last ten years of his life, Florence kept Hardy within an ever more limited circle. 'I think I would rather strangers (even great admirers) did not come to see him now,' she wrote to Cockerell. T. E. Lawrence was a regular and welcome visitor from camp at Bovington and his retreat nearby at Clouds Hill. He found Hardy unbelievably composed: '. . . the standards of the man!' he wrote to Robert Graves in 1923. 'He feels interest in everyone and veneration for no-one. I've not found in him any bowing-down, moral or material or spiritual. . . . He is waiting so tranquilly for death.'

Hardy the local curiosity: laying the foundation stone of the new buildings at Dorchester Grammar School on 21 July 1927. Hardy made an uncharacteristically long speech, mainly about the school's founder, his putative ancestor, Thomas Hardy of Melcombe Regis.

After a visit to Oxford in June 1923, Hardy never slept away from Max Gate. On public appearances, like the visit of the Prince of Wales to Dorchester to open a drill hall for the yeomanry or laying the foundation stone of the new buildings of Dorchester Grammar School, he seemed ever more remote and self-contained. When he wrote 'Nobody Comes' in 1924 he may, for the first time in his life, have been in deeper seclusion than he really desired, but he did not worry about it as Florence evidently did when she reported the following conversation:

F: It's twelve days since you spoke to anyone outside the house.
H: I have spoken to someone.
F: Who was it?
H: The man who drove the manure cart.
F: What did you say?
H: 'Good Morning.'

By 1926, Hardy admitted to being weary of his work and began

The path at the edge of Kingston Maurward park, looking towards Dorchester.

to sink contentedly into the reflective calm of extreme age. Until the last six weeks, he was able to dictate the pace of his farewell to life. In the winter of 1926-7 he could still retrace on foot the ground he loved best, over to Stinsford and beside the Frome. In the evenings he sat over the fire with Florence, running over his earliest memories and the watersheds in his life. The very first was of the concertina his father had given him when he was four, the frozen fieldfare and how he once pretended to eat grass in a field of sheep to see what they would do and looked up to find them gathered round him, gazing open-mouthed. He remembered his arguments with Bastow and told Florence that if he could live his life again he would prefer to be an obscure architect in a country town, like John Hicks.

In November 1927 he told Florence that he had done all he wanted to do and three weeks later sat down at his desk and found himself for the first time unable to work. By Christmas he was confined to bed, where his mind began gradually to weaken with his body. At

dusk on 11 January he asked Florence to read him a verse from *Omar Khayyám*:

> Oh, Thou, who Man of baser Earth didst make,
> And ev'n with Paradise devise the Snake:
>   For all the Sin wherewith the Face of Man
> Is blacken'd – Man's forgiveness give – and take!

Shortly after nine he died.

'I do not, in truth, feel *much* interest in posthumous opinions about me', Hardy wrote in 1914, 'and shall sleep quite calmly at Stinsford whatever happens.' But only his heart was buried in Emma's grave. The rest of the frail body which had almost escaped life on his mother's bed at Bockhampton was burnt and the ashes lodged in the stoniest soil in England at Westminster Abbey. No doubt the double funeral would have ranked high in Hardy's catalogue of the bizarre.

*If not in years; of manner cold;*
*Who seemed as stone,*
*And never had known*
*Of mirth or moan.*

*And there may have crossed your path a lover,*
*In whose clear depths you could discover*
*A staunch, robust,*
*And tender trust,*
*Through storm and gust.*

*And you may have also known one fickle,*
*Whose fancies changed as the silver sickle*
*Of yonder moon,*
*Which shapes so soon*
*To demilune!*

*You entertained a person once*
*Whom you internally deemed a dunce:—*
*As he sat in view*
*Just facing you*
*You saw him through.*

*You came to know a learned seer*
*Of whom you read the surface mere:*
*Your soul quite sank;*
*Brain of such rank*
*Dubbed yours a blank.*

*Anon you quizzed a man of sadness,*
*Who never could have known true gladness*
*Just for a whim*
*You pitied him*
*In his sore trim.*

*You journeyed with a man so glad*
*You never could conceive him sad:*
*He proved to be*
*Indubitably*
*Good company.*

*You lit on an unadventurous slow man,*
*Who, said you, need be feared by no man;*
*That his slack deeds*
*And sloth must needs*
*Produce but weeds.*

*A man of enterprise, shrewd and swift,*
*Who never suffered affairs to drift,*
*You eyed for a time*
*Just in his prime,*
*And judged he might climb.*

*You smoked beside one who forgot*
*All that you said, or grasped it not.*
*Quite a poor thing,*
*Not worth a sting*
*By satirizing!*

*Next year you nearly lost for ever*
*Goodwill from one who forgot slights never;*
*And, with unease,*
*Felt you must seize*
*Occasion to please . . .*

*Now . . . . All these specimens of man,*
*So various in their pith and plan,*
*Curious to say*
*Were* one *man. Yea,*
*I was all they.*

HERE LIES THE HEART OF
THOMAS·HARDY·O·M
ON·OF·THOMAS AND JEMIMA HARDY
BORN AT UPPER BOCKHAMPTON·2 JUNE·1840
ED AT MAX·GATE DORCHESTER 11 JANUARY·1928
ES·REST·IN·POETS·CORNER WESTMINSTER·ABBEY

**Black and White Illustrations**

*Abbreviations* DCM: Dorset County Museum, Dorchester. NMR: National Monuments Record, London. RTHPL: Radio Times, Hulton Picture Library. ML: Macmillan London Ltd. NPG: National Portrait Gallery, London. S-C: Photographs by Hermann Lea and others in the possession of James and Gregory Stevens-Cox, editors of *The Thomas Hardy Year Book*. Cooke: Photographs by Hermann Lea and the Rev Thomas Perkins in the possession of Robert Cooke, M.P., of Athelhampton, Dorset.

## Bibliography

### 1. Hardy's Major Works

1865 'How I Built Myself a House'
1871 *Desperate Remedies*
1872 *Under the Greenwood Tree*
1873 *A Pair of Blue Eyes*
1874 *Far from the Madding Crowd*
1876 *The Hand of Ethelberta*
1878 *The Return of the Native*
1880 *The Trumpet-Major*
1881 *A Laodicean*
1822 *Two on a Tower*
1883 'The Dorsetshire Labourer'
1886 *The Mayor of Casterbridge*
1887 *The Woodlanders*
1888 *Wessex Tales*
'The Profitable Reading of Fiction'
1890 'Candour in English Fiction'
1891 *A Group of Noble Dames*
'The Science of Fiction'
*Tess of the d'Urbervilles*
1892 'Why I Don't Write Plays'
1894 *Life's Little Ironies*
1896 *Jude the Obscure*
1897 *The Well-Beloved*
1898 *Wessex Poems*
1902 *Poems of the Past and the Present*
1903 *The Dynasts*, Part I
1905 *The Dynasts*, Part II
1906 'Memories of Church Restoration'
1908 *The Dynasts*, Part III
'Dorset in London'
1909 *Time's Laughingstocks*
1912 'A Plea for Pure English'
1913 *A Changed Man*
1914 *Satires of Circumstance*
1917 *Moments of Vision*
1922 *Late Lyrics and Earlier*
1923 *The Famous Tragedy of the Queen of Cornwall*
1925 *Human Shows*
1928 *Winter Words*
F. E. Hardy, *The Early Life of Thomas Hardy, 1840–1891*
1930 F. E. Hardy, *The Later Years of Thomas Hardy, 1892–1928*

*The Complete Poems*, ed. James Gibson; and *Collected Stories*, ed. F. B. Pinion.

*The Dynasts* has been reissued on one volume, with an introduction by John Wain (Macmillan, 1965); and the *Early Life* and the *Later Years* have been reissued as *The Life of Thomas Hardy, 1840–1928* (Macmillan, 1962). A miscellany containing such items as *The Famous Tragedy of the Queen of Cornwall*, the children's pieces and the previously uncollected short stories is in preparation.

Hardy's non-fiction prose works are collected in *Thomas Hardy's Personal Writings*, ed. Harold Orel (Macmillan, 1967).

**2. Biography**

The principal published sources for Hardy's life are:

*The Architectural Notebook of Thomas Hardy*, ed. C. J. P. Beatty (Dorset Natural History and Archaeological Society, 1966).

*'Dearest Emmie'*, ed. Carl J. Weber (Macmillan, 1963). Surviving letters from Hardy to his first wife.

*Friends of a Lifetime*, ed. Viola Meynell (Cape, 1940). Pages 274–315 consist of letters of Hardy and Florence to Sir Sydney Cockerell, 1911–27.

Hardy, Emma, *Some Recollections*, ed. Evelyn Hardy and Robert Gittings (Oxford University Press, 1961).

Hardy, Florence Emily, *The Life of Thomas Hardy, 1840–1928* (Macmillan, 1962). A large part of the *Life* consists of Hardy's own selections from his diaries, notebooks and letters.

*Monographs on the Life of Thomas Hardy*, ed. James Stevens-Cox, nos 1–72 (Toucan Press, 1962–70); continued in *The Thomas Hardy Year Book*, ed. James and Gregory Stevens-Cox (Toucan Press, 1970– ). Not all are strictly sources. Some are essays of a very controversial nature by contemporary Hardy scholars, but the monographs include reminiscences of Hardy by people who knew and worked for him.

*One Rare Fair Woman*, ed. Evelyn Hardy and F. B. Pinion (Macmillan, 1972). Hardy's letters to the Hon. Florence Henniker, 1893–1922.

*Thomas Hardy's Notebooks*, ed. Evelyn Hardy (Hogarth Press, 1955).

New and complete editions of Hardy's letters and notebooks are in preparation.

*annotated bibliography of writings about him*, ed. Helmut E. Gerber and W. Eugene Davis (Northern Illinois University Press, 1973).

The principal reference books and works on the major aspects of Hardy's life and work are:

Bailey, J. O., *The Poetry of Thomas Hardy* (University of North Carolina Press, 1970).

Kay-Robinson, Denys, *Hardy's Wessex Reappraised* (David & Charles, 1972).

Millgate, Michael, *Thomas Hardy: his career as a novelist* (Bodley Head, 1971).

Pinion, F. B., *A Hardy Companion*, revised ed. (Macmillan, 1974).

Purdy, R. L., *Thomas Hardy: a bibliographical study* (Oxford University Press, 1954; reissued 1968).

*Thomas Hardy: the critical heritage*, ed. R. G. Cox (Routledge & Kegan Paul, 1970).

Of the numerous general books on Hardy, the most sensitive biography is Evelyn Hardy's *Thomas Hardy* (Hogarth Press, 1954) and the most refreshing critical survey J. I. M. Stewart's *Thomas Hardy* (Longman, 1971).

Robert Gitting's *Young Thomas Hardy* (Heinemann Educational Books, 1975), containing much detail about Hardy's early life, appeared while the present book was in the press.

## Index

*Note: References in italics are to illustrations or captions. Textual references may appear on the same pages.*

Fictitious names as Exonbury
Real names as Portsmouth
Isles of Lyonnesse
S. Maria
Giant's Town
Beeny or Cliff without name
Targan Bay
Valleney Vale
Endelstow
Dundagel
Castle Boterel
Bariwith Strand
OFF WESSEX
Trufal
Redrutin
Penzephyr
Lands End
Bristol Channel
Bristol
Heymere House
Mendip Hills
Prospect Hotel
Stancy Castle
Cliff Martin
Exon Moor
Dunkery Beacon
Quantock Hills
Will's Neck
Poldon Hills
Fountall
Glaston
Marshal's Elm
Sedgemoor
Downstaple
Toneborough Deane
River Parret
Toneborough
Ivelchester
Ivell
Tivworthy
LOWER WESSEX
Exe Valley
Silverthorn
River Otter
River Axe
Emminster
King's Hintock
Evershead
Crimmercrock Lane
Chalk Newton
Pilsdon
Toller Down
SOUTH
Casterbridge
Exonbury
Idmouth
Port Bredy
Deadmans Bay
Blackon
Waddon Vale
Pebble Bank
Street of Wells
Isle of Slingers
The Beal
Tor-upon-Sea